Leaders
from the
Kitchen

A window into the kitchens of
Belizean and Nicaraguan women who
lead (and feed) their communities

D1571465

Proceeds from this book benefit
women's economic and professional
development in Belize & Nicaragua

Progresso, Belize: Women dish up escabeche and sweet potato pudding at a community potluck honoring mothers who participate in the local 4-H club.

This book is dedicated to the everyday women leaders in Belize and Nicaragua who nourish their communities in visible and invisible ways.

Funding for this project was provided in part by the U.S. Department of State for a program called "Development of Grassroots Organizations for Women: An Exchange Program for Emerging Leaders in Nicaragua, Belize and the U.S." implemented by Citizen Bridges International (formerly Heartland International) in Chicago, in partnership with WIN Belize in Belize City and Casa Alianza-Nicaragua in Managua.

Published by Leaders from the Kitchen Press, 2012

COPYRIGHT NOTICE

Printed in the United States of America on acid-free paper.

15 14 13 12   4 3 2 1

Library of Congress Control Number:

ISBN 978-0-615-88209-3

This project is supported by Citizen Bridges International (Chicago), Casa Alianza-Nicaragua (Managua), and WIN Belize (Belize City) and funded in part with a grant from the U.S. Department of State.

Proceeds Notice: Proceeds from this cookbook will support the professional and leadership development of Belizean and Nicaraguan women like the ones profiled in this book. See page 9 for more details.

Cover Image Caption: A woman sells moronga and empanadas streetside in Bluefields, Nicaragua.

Cover and Interior designer: Jessica Huang

Photography: Megan Hryndza, Carlos Olivas, Sarah Sumadi, Jason Kaumeyer

Table of Contents

INTRODUCTION, p. 7
How this project began, p. 8
Our partner organizations, p. 9
A little bit about Belize, p. 10
A little bit about Nicaragua, p. 11

RECIPES, p. 13

BREAKFASTS, p. 14
Gallo Pinto (Black Beans and Rice), p. 16
Huevos Revueltos (Scrambled Eggs) with
　Chorizo and Avocado, p. 18
Powder Buns, p. 20
Garden Tofu Quiche with Vegetables, p. 21
Johnny Cakes (Breakfast Biscuits), p. 22
Coconut Milk Pancakes with Bananas and
　Walnuts, p. 23

STARTERS AND SNACKS, p. 24
Mini Pizzas, p. 27
Salbutes (Fried Tortillas with Chicken,
　Tomatoes and Cabbage), p. 28
Garnachas (Tostadas with Beans), p. 29
Enchiladas (Fried Empanadas filled with
　Meat and Rice), p. 30
Guacamole with Hard-Boiled Eggs, p. 33
Shrimp Ceviche, p. 33

SOUPS AND STEWS P. 36
Hudut with Falumou (Garifuna Fish and
　Coconut Stew with Mashed Plantains),
　p. 38
Sopa de Albóndigas (Chicken and Squash
　Meatball Stew), p. 40
Indio Viejo (Beef and Vegetable Stew),
　p. 41
Chimole (Black Stew), p. 42
Split Peas and Pig Tails, p. 44
Run Down (Caribbean Soup of Meat,
　Coconut Milk and Vegetables), p. 45
Escabeche (Spicy Stew with Chicken
　and Onions), p. 46

SALADS AND SIDES, p. 48
Pilau Rice, p. 50
Potato and Egg Salad, p. 52
Darasa (Garifuna Banana and Coconut
　Dumplings), p. 53
Maduros en Gloria (Sweet Baked
　Plantains), p. 54
Crispy Fried Plantain Chips, p. 57
Crunchy Corn Tortillas, p. 58
Flour Tortillas, p. 58
Coconut Rice and Beans, p. 60

DINNERS, p. 62
Spicy Chicken Tamales wrapped in
　Banana Leaves, p. 67
Red Recado Spice Blend, p. 68
Carne Asada, p. 69
Stew Chicken, p. 70
Arroz de la Valenciana (Rice with Chicken
　and Vegetables), p. 71
Vigorón (Fried Yucca topped with Fried
　Pork Rind and Cabbage Slaw), p. 72
Baked Curry Chicken, p. 73
Grilled Garlic-Lime Snapper, p. 73
Frito (Fried Chicken atop Tangy Cabbage
　Slaw and Plantain Chips), p. 74

SWEETS AND DRINKS, p. 76
Pudín de Camote (Sweet Potato Pudding),
　p. 78
Horchata (Sweet Rice Milk Drink), p. 80
Fresco de Cacao (Chocolate Rice Milk
　Drink), p. 81
Coffee Flan, p. 82
Ginger Hibiscus Punch, p. 83
Blonde Fudge, p. 84
Tres Leches Cake, p. 86
Progresso Bread Pudding, p. 87
Pastel de Quequisque (Taro Root Cake),
　p. 88
Macúa de Nicaragua (Rum Cocktail), p. 89
Papaya Punch, p. 89
Pio Quinto, p. 90

Above: Freshly-made tortillas being sold in a
market in Bluefields, Nicaragua.

Cabbage, sweet potato, cassava, limes, and
potatoes for sale at Belize City's central market.

Opposite page: Salbutes with a finishing touch
of sliced tomatoes.

**EAT, SHARE, GET INVOLVED,
　p. 93**
Bringing Nutrition to Every Family:
　Addressing Food Security in Nicaragua
　and Belize, p. 95
4-H at work in Progresso, Belize, p. 96
WIN Belize at work in Belize City, Belize,
　p. 97
Other organizations advancing women's
　rights in Belize, p. 97
Fabretto Children's Foundation at work
　across Nicaragua, p. 98
OMAN at work in Bluefields, Nicaragua,
　p. 99
Other organizations advancing women's
　rights in Nicaragua, p. 99

RECIPE INDEX, p. 101

ACKNOWLEDGEMENTS, p. 103

MEET THE PROJECT TEAM, p. 104

A young girl waves from the window of her home in the Jane Usher Boulevard area of Belize City, Belize.

Introduction

If you don't know Belizean or Nicaraguan cuisine, or you haven't eaten it lately, dig in with us.

Belize and Nicaragua are home to culinary traditions that represent a proud and diverse cross-section of Central American cuisine, blending Caribbean, Creole, Garifuna, indigenous, Spanish, and Mestizo flavors. From gallo pinto, a traditional dish of rice and black beans, to escabeche, a spicy chicken and onion stew, to the decadent tres leches cake, the many flavors of Belize and Nicaragua have won the adoration of fans across the world.

Leaders from the Kitchen is a window into the lives – and kitchens – of Belizean and Nicaraguan women who are starting businesses, creating jobs, building schools, advancing women's rights, and furthering economic equity.

Why focus on women? Women are responsible for 60-80% of the world's food production and nearly 100% of food preparation. Yet they earn just 10% of the world's income and own just 2% of the world's land. At a global level, women's labor is overlooked and undervalued, and this gender discrimination limits women's access to education, credit, and leadership positions. Leaders from the Kitchen shares stories of women advancing opportunities for other women. In doing so, we hope to add to their efforts to create new opportunities and inspiration for women's leadership.

100% of the proceeds from this cookbook support the economic and professional development of low-income and at-risk emerging women leaders in Nicaragua and Belize. Women like Lilia Ack from Progresso, Belize, who prepares hundreds of tamales from dusk until dawn to cater breakfasts at community events (p. 67). You'll meet women like Debora Espinosa Arce, a budding micro-entrepreneur from Bluefields, Nicaragua, who sells enchiladas out of her home while supporting victims of domestic violence and raising her little girl (p. 75).

In this book you'll also meet established women leaders who are giving back, like Doña Pinita, Nicaragua's first female celebrity chef. She owns a leading restaurant in Managua and built her enterprise by giving at-risk women their first shot in the workforce (p. 81).

Our Leaders from the Kitchen have shared their favorite foods and their stories. Thanks for joining us at the table.

How this project began

The Leaders From the Kitchen cookbook began in Chicago in November 2011 as part of a leadership development and exchange program called "From the Ground Up," funded by the U.S. Department of State and implemented by Citizen Bridges International. The program brought together 60 young women leaders working in nonprofit and social enterprise sectors in Belize, Nicaragua, and the United States to develop projects to improve the lives of women and youth in Belize and Nicaragua.

Eight of us stepped forward to focus on women's economic development. And so began the collaboration and friendship of Daisy, Indira, Jamie H., Jamie P., Lestell, Marcela, Megan and Sarah – and the idea for this cookbook.

Our team comes from both large cities and rural areas in Belize, Nicaragua, and the U.S. We speak Creole, English and Spanish. Our ethnic backgrounds include Afro-Caribbean, European, Garifuna, Mestizo and Middle Eastern. We have professional experience in domestic violence prevention,

psychotherapy, counseling, housing and economic development, labor rights, microfinance, advocacy, journalism, marketing and design.

Why focus on women's economic development? Studies have shown that women's empowerment raises economic productivity, reduces infant and maternal mortality, and increases young girls' access to education. Our team of eight has firsthand experience in working to support women's leadership.

In Managua, Nicaragua, Marcela witnessed the importance of economic opportunity in transforming the lives of three young women at a jewelry-making cooperative (see stories p. 40 and p. 71). From Chicago, Megan produced a global documentary about microfinance and learned how media could help advance the coexistence of business and social development. On Nicaragua's Atlantic coast, Lestell worked with domestic violence survivors and saw that what often prevented women from leaving abusive situations was a lack of economic opportunity (see p. 75). Jamie P. worked as a social worker in

Chicago and observed that support was more effective when women became financially independent. In Progresso, Belize, Daisy saw that women's work in subsistence farming was critical to feeding their families (see p. 79). Indira, in Belize City, transformed unemployed women in her community into makers of school uniforms (see p. 50). Following her work as a labor rights advocate in Chicago, Jamie Hayes launched her own clothing design business and seeks to support fair labor practices abroad. Sarah has worked as an advocate for the rights of minorities and LGBT people, and as a volunteer coordinator, saw that committed individuals could help change the world.

Leaning upon our collective experience, we envision a future where more women have the resources and know-how to be leaders in their communities. In piloting the Leaders from the Kitchen cookbook, we hope to share a slice of Belizean and Nicaraguan cuisine while building awareness, support, and investment for women's business and leadership development. Please eat, drink, learn, and share the goodness.

This page: Debora's kitchen (see story, p. 75) in Bluefields, Nicaragua. Right: Lilia's kitchen (see story, p. 67) in Progresso, Belize.

Your purchase of this cookbook benefits the following partner organizations.

100% of the proceeds from this cookbook will support women's economic and professional development in each of the Kitchen Leaders' communities featured in this book: Belize City and Progresso (Belize) and Bluefields and Managua (Nicaragua). The proceeds will be channeled through the following organizations:

IN NICARAGUA

Fabretto Children's Foundation: Fabretto empowers underserved children and their families in Nicaragua to improve their livelihoods and increase their economic opportunities through education, nutrition, and professional development. One of Fabretto's many projects is the NicaHOPE jewelry program, which teaches jewelry-making to over 60 young women from the area in and around La Chureca, Managua's city trash dump.

OMAN: OMAN, the Organización de Mujeres Afrodescendientes de Nicaragua (Organization of Nicaraguan Women of African Descent), works to promote the identity, culture and traditions of the Afro-descendant population of the Caribbean coast of Nicaragua. OMAN involves young women in the community to advocate for a variety of social justice causes, including economic development, women's entrepreneurship and empowerment, and ending violence against women.

IN BELIZE

4-H Youth Development Center: 4-H provides vocational training, personal development and life skills training, entrepreneurial support, job placement assistance and agricultural education to youth ages 14-17. Since public high schools in Belize are not free, 4-H also helps young adults attend school, fundraising throughout the year to offer scholarships. Most 4-H participants come from single-parent homes, and their mothers volunteer to support the program.

WIN (Women's Issues Network) Belize: WIN Belize advocates for women's rights, empowers women economically and strengthens local organizations through fundraising and staff training. WIN Belize led a successful campaign to raise the minimum wage for jobs largely occupied by women, and is currently working to empower more women to run for office.

To learn more about our beneficiary organizations or other ways to help leading community organizations in Belize and Nicaragua to advance women's equity, see page 93.

A little bit about Belize

This tiny country, about the size of New Hampshire with a quarter of the population, is an extremely diverse society comprised of multiple cultures including Mestizo, Garifuna, and Creole. Belizeans are multilingual – nearly all speak Creole and English, and most speak Spanish as a third language.

Belizean cuisine combines Caribbean, Mexican and Spanish cooking, and varies from the north to the south. Fish and shellfish are abundant, and the tropical landscape provides plentiful fruits like plantains, mangoes, bananas, papayas and coconuts. Belizean meals vary from simple staples like rice and beans cooked in coconut milk to heartier stews such as Chimole or Hudut Baruru with Falumou, a popular Garifuna dish made of fish and coconut.

Tourists have long flocked to Belize's coastline and its more than 450 cayes (tiny islands). Areas like San Pedro and Placencia Beach are lined with resort hotels and are popular destinations for cruise ships. But Belize is more than just a pretty beach – the country's astounding ecodiversity lends itself to some of the best scuba diving and snorkeling

in the world, and tourists can go birdwatching, ride a zipline or catch a glimpse of the elusive manatee. The interior of the country, which remains largely ignored by visitors, contains other treasures. Small Mennonite communities are found all over Belize, and their German-speaking members make their living farming and raising dairy cattle.

Despite its status as a tourist's tropical paradise, the reality of life for most Belizeans isn't as rosy. Unemployment is high, especially among women. Education continues to be an obstacle for many families – only primary school education is compulsory, and public high schools are not free. As a result, only about 38% of Belizean youth attend high school. More than a third of Belizeans live below the poverty line.

Organizations like the Women's Issues Network (WIN Belize) and the 4-H Youth Development Center are working to make change, empower women and increase their educational and economic opportunities. Read on to meet some of the women who have been supported by these programs, and discover how they're giving back to their communities.

A little bit about Nicaragua

Nicaragua is too often defined by its tragedies and setbacks. During the 1970s, '80s and '90s, the country experienced near-constant political unrest and violence, a massive earthquake, and Hurricanes Juana and Mitch. In just 30 years, Nicaragua was decimated, and the country is still recovering from both the man-made and natural destruction. After Haiti, Nicaragua remains the second-poorest country in the Western hemisphere.

But Nicaragua is slowly rebuilding itself – and more and more people are finding out about the rich landscape and diverse cultural heritage that have long existed here. In the last 10 years, income from tourism has risen more than 300 percent, making tourism Nicaragua's largest industry. Nicaragua is dotted with volcanoes, lakes, jungles and beaches. Protected nature reserves house more than 20 percent of Nicaraguan land, home to millions of species of plants and wildlife. The two largest freshwater lakes in Central America – Lake Managua and Lake Nicaragua – are found here. It's no wonder the indigenous Nahuatl-speaking tribe, who inhabited the land before the Spanish arrived, named their land "nicarao," meaning "surrounded by water."

Nicaragua's 5.7 million residents are largely a mix of Mestizos, descendants of Spanish and indigenous peoples. The official language is Spanish, although English and Creole are widely spoken on the Atlantic coast. Nicaraguan cuisine relies heavily on rice, beans, corn, plantains, chicken and pork. Seafood is popular along the Caribbean coast, where a bourgeoning fishing industry harvests tons of shrimp and spiny lobster each year. There's an array of tropical fruits available, including papaya, coconut, mango, passion-fruit, and avocado. Starchy roots like yucca and cassava are also common. Coffee, grown in the cooler highlands of the north, is Nicaragua's top export. Many say Nicaragua's Flor de Caña rum is the best in Latin America.

Nicaragua faces many challenges – 79% of its citizens still live on less than $2 per day, and as in many developing countries, women bear the brunt of economic disadvantage. But organizations like the Fabretto Children's Foundation and OMAN – beneficiaries of this book – are working to improve economic and educational opportunities for all Nicaraguans. Read on to discover many traditional Nicaraguan recipes from women leaders who are helping to lead local economic activity.

QUICK FACTS

BELIZE

Capital: Belmopan
Population: 327,719
Pop. below poverty line: 43%
Unemployment rate: 13.1%
Languages spoken: English (official), Spanish, Mayan, Garifuna, Creole
Did you know? The Belize Barrier Reef is the largest in the Western Hemisphere, and second in the world after Australia's Great Barrier Reef.

NICARAGUA

Capital: Managua
Population: 5,727,707
Pop. below poverty line: 46.2%
Unemployment rate: 8.6%
Languages spoken: Spanish (official); Miskito, Creole and indigenous languages spoken on Atlantic coast
Did you know? The Indio Maiz Biological Reserve has more species of birds, trees and insects than all of Europe.

Recipes

Fried plantains
(p. 57) and the
tamale-making
process in
Progresso, Belize
(p. 67).

Breakfasts

Left, clockwise:
Students in San
Isidro, Nicaragua,
eat a nutritious
lunch provided by
Fabretto (p. 17),
Johnny Cakes (p.
22), freshly-grated
coconut.

Gallo pinto is often eaten for breakfast in Nicaragua, but it works well as a side dish to any meal.

Gallo Pinto (Black Beans and Rice)

Teresa Garcia Flores and Katty Vasquez Nicaragua, San Isidro, Nicaragua

1 cup rice
½ cup dried black beans
1 small onion, finely chopped
½ a red bell pepper, finely chopped
1 garlic clove, crushed
Vegetable oil for cooking
Salt to taste

Rinse the beans and soak them overnight in several cups of water to soften them. Boil the beans in water to cover by two inches along with the garlic. When the beans are tender, drain them and set them aside, reserving the water the beans were cooked in. Salt to taste.

Sauté the onions and peppers in oil in a large pan until soft. Cook the rice on low heat in approximately 2 cups of the black bean broth. When most of the water has evaporated, lower the heat and cover the rice, cooking for 5 minutes more.

Add the beans to the sautéed onions and peppers, and sauté for a few minutes together. Add the rice and mix well. Add a little more bean broth if you need, and cook a few minutes more. Note: Some people prefer their gallo pinto softer, others more fried. For softer rice, add more bean broth. For a crispier taste, add more oil and fry the gallo pinto longer at the end. Serve warm.

Serves 4.

Thanks to Katty and Teresa for contributing their recipe and supporting women leaders in Belize and Nicaragua.

Teresa Garcia Flores (L) and Katty Vasquez Nicaragua (R) at work in a school cafeteria in San Isidro, Nicaragua.

Katty and Teresa work tirelessly to provide nutritious and delicious school lunches to children in the rural village of San Isidro, outside Managua. The Fabretto Children's Foundation supports the lunch program, which relies on a combination of low-cost, nutrient-rich ingredients like locally-grown vegetables, soy and eggs, and the creativity of chefs like Katty and Teresa.

Lunch at school is crucial – it's often the only meal the children eat every day, and many of them save part of their lunch to share with their siblings at dinner. Since Katty and Teresa started providing healthy lunches five years ago, they've seen great results. Over the course of each school year, students gain weight, pay more attention in class and learn better. "We've seen a real change in these children," Katty says. "The best part is, we make for them what we would eat ourselves: a meal made with love and care."

Their recipes are award-winning. Last year they entered a national recipe contest where Katty's recipe for Garden Tofu Quiche (p. 21) won first prize.

Huevos Revueltos (Scrambled Eggs) with Chorizo and Avocado

Esperanza Pereira, Managua, Nicaragua

1 onion, diced
1 tomato, diced and seeded
1 habanero pepper, diced
6 eggs
1 cup chorizo or bacon, diced
Vegetable oil for cooking
Salt and pepper to taste
1 avocado

In a pan, sauté the onions with a tablespoon or two of oil. Add the tomato and habanero peppers, and sauté until they soften. Add the chorizo or bacon and cook until browned, stirring regularly. Add eggs, salt and pepper and scramble, stirring to prevent sticking. Serve with gallo pinto (see p. 16) and a couple of slices of avocado on the side.

Serves 4.

Thanks to Esperanza Pereira of Managua for contributing her recipe and supporting women leaders in Belize and Nicaragua.

Powder Buns

Carolyn West, Belize City, Belize

2 ½ cups flour
1 cup brown sugar
¼ teaspoon baking powder
pinch of salt
pinch of nutmeg
4 tablespoons shortening
½ teaspoon of vanilla
3/4 cups coconut milk

In a bowl, combine flour, sugar, baking powder, nutmeg, and salt. Add shortening, vanilla, and coconut milk, and mix and knead well. Roll the dough into little balls, and flatten them so they look like puffy pancakes. Grease the baking sheet with a little shortening, and place dough balls on the baking sheet. Bake at 375 degrees until brown, approximately 15-20 minutes.

Yields 14-18 buns.

Thanks to Carolyn West for contributing her recipe and supporting women leaders in Belize and Nicaragua.

Carolyn is a preschool teacher at the King Jesus Preschool in the Jane Usher Boulevard area in Belize City, a zone that suffers from gang violence. Carolyn has kept the school open for years despite financial struggles and some families' inability to pay school fees.

Garden Tofu Quiche with Vegetables

Katty Vasquez Nicaragua, San Isidro, Nicaragua

This recipe won first prize in a national recipe contest.

1 cup rice
1 cup firm tofu
½ cup finely chopped tomatoes
1 cup finely chopped onions
½ a green pepper, finely chopped
1 garlic clove, finely chopped
½ celery stalk, finely chopped
A few sprigs cilantro, finely chopped
3 eggs
Vegetable oil for frying
Squeeze of lemon juice
Salt and pepper to taste

Cook the rice according to package instructions, and set aside to cool. Place the tofu in a bowl of cold water for 10 minutes, then drain. In a pot, boil enough water to cover the tofu. Once boiling, place the tofu into the pot and immediately reduce heat to low. Let the tofu cook for 10 minutes, then drain and let cool.

In a bowl, mix the cooked rice, tofu and chopped raw vegetables. Add the eggs one at a time, then the salt, pepper and lemon juice. Whisk well until egg is blended. Heat oil in a frying pan and pour in the mixture. Fry until golden brown and solid. Serve warm.

Serves 4.

Thanks to Katty for contributing her recipe and supporting women leaders in Belize and Nicaragua.

Johnny Cakes are biscuits made from a simple flour dough and are often cooked over an open flame. They were originally called Journey Cakes because they would stay fresh for weeks and could be packed as sustenance for long journeys.

Johnny Cakes (Breakfast Biscuits)

Daisy Magaña, Progresso, Belize

2 cups white flour
2 tablespoons shortening
2 tablespoons butter
1 ½ teaspoons baking powder
Pinch of salt
½ cup coconut milk
½ cup of water, if necessary

Combine the flour, baking powder and salt. Add butter and shortening to dry ingredients. Stir in coconut milk gradually, kneading the dough until the lumps disappear, adding the ½ cup of water if necessary.

Shape into round balls, approximately the size of golf balls. Place the dough

balls into a bowl and cover with a damp towel and let sit for an hour.

Place on a greased baking sheet. Flatten lightly and poke a few holes in each with a fork.

Bake until golden brown at 425 degrees, about 15 minutes. Serve with butter. Can also be used to make delicious breakfast sandwiches with meat, cheese or eggs.

Yields 12-14 Johnny Cakes.

Thanks to Daisy Magaña for contributing her recipe and supporting women leaders in Belize and Nicaragua.

Coconut Milk Pancakes with Bananas and Walnuts

Chef Esther, Changes in Latitudes Bed and and Breakfast, San Pedro, Belize

2 cups milk
1 can coconut milk
2 cups oatmeal
1 stick butter
2 eggs
1/2 cup flour
1/2 teaspoon cinnamon
2 tablespoons sugar
2 teaspoons baking powder
Dash of paprika and ground cloves
1/2 cup crushed walnuts
1/2 cup raisins
1/2 cup grated coconut
1/2 can sweetened condensed milk
1-2 tablespoons pancake syrup

PANCAKES

Mix milk, coconut milk, oatmeal, butter, eggs, flour, cinnamon, sugar, baking powder, paprika and cloves together into a batter. Heat vegetable oil in a pan, and fry approximately ¼ cups' worth of batter for each pancake.

CARAMEL TOPPING

Heat one can of condensed milk on low heat. When melted, mix with a little pancake syrup, walnuts, raisins and grated coconut. Serve the pancakes warm with the topping.

Yields 10 pancakes.

Thanks to Chef Esther for contributing her recipe and supporting women leaders in Belize and Nicaragua.

Top: Plantains hang outside an outdoor kitchen in Progresso, Belize. Bottom: Hand-grated coconut.

Starters & S

nacks

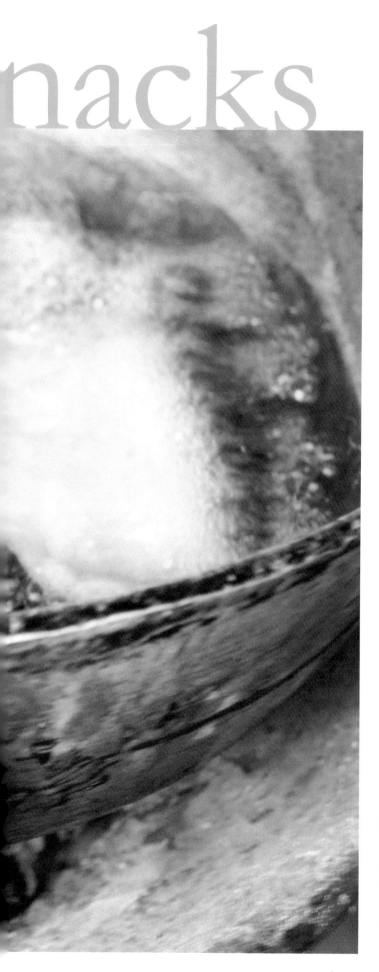

Left, clockwise:
Nicaraguan
enchiladas frying
(p. 30), street
food in Belize and
Nicaragua (p. 34),
and Doña Pinita's
guacamole (p. 33).

Mini Pizzas

Nicole Simone Bethrun, Belize City, Belize

DOUGH

3 cups flour
1 package dry yeast
½ teaspoon salt
1 cup warm water
2 tablespoons vegetable or olive oil

TOPPINGS

1 sweet bell pepper, chopped
1 medium onion, chopped
2 cloves garlic, crushed
1 can tomato sauce
Pepperoni or ground beef
Mozzarella cheese, shredded

In a large mixing bowl, combine 1 ¼ cups flour, yeast, salt, warm water, and oil. Fold with spoon or beat with whisk or electric mixer. Stir in the remaining flour. Knead the dough on a smooth surface until moderately stiff, smooth and elastic. Cover with a towel or wrap in plastic wrap and let it rise for 1 hour. Dough yields 1 medium pizza or 4 mini pizzas.

While the dough is rising, preheat the oven to 425 degrees and prepare the toppings. Nicole's family uses minced bell peppers, onion, garlic and tomato sauce, but almost any toppings can be used. Nicole's family will often substitute cooked ground beef, minced hot dog sausage, or even chicken lunchmeat for pepperoni, which can be very expensive in Belize.

After the dough has risen, place the dough on a floured cutting board or counter, punch it down, and shape the dough into 6-inch circles. Roll out each circle and place on the greased baking sheet. Press the edges of the dough with a fork (optional). Spread the tomato sauce over the crusts, sprinkle the cheese on top and add toppings.

Bake at 425 degrees until lightly browned, about 15-20 minutes.

Serves 4.

kitchen leader

100% of the proceeds from this book benefit the economic and professional development of women like Nicole.

Although Nicole currently owns a small pastry shop, she's beginning to expand her skills beyond the kitchen. Since she's always had a knack for gardening, Nicole recently secured a plot of land near her home with the hopes of starting a small nursery to sell flowers and plants. With the financial support of her mother, who lives and works in the U.S., Nicole has been able to collect seeds and fertilizer to help grow her enterprise.

While working as a restaurant cook, Nicole invented this recipe and then modified it, using local and cheaper ingredients to make it at home. Now, every Saturday evening is "pizza night," and Nicole, her husband and six children make and enjoy her recipe together.

Norma is the single mother of five children. She's a fabulous cook, and supports her family by baking bread, tostadas, pies and other sweets and selling them around the neighborhood. Right now, she sends her children door-to-door with baskets of sweets to sell, but she hopes to save enough money to open a small stand outside her house so her children can focus on school.

Norma is now a single parent – when her husband became abusive a few years ago, she went to the Department of Human Services for assistance in keeping her children safe and supporting them alone. "As a woman, I feel proud of myself because I have survived," Norma said.

"We women have the strength to succeed, with or without a companion. We just need to be creative and make opportunities for ourselves." Norma's salbutes are one of her most sought-after recipes.

Salbutes (Fried Tortillas with Chicken, Tomatoes and Cabbage)

Norma Ondina Soliz, Progresso, Belize

CRUNCHY CORN TORTILLAS
8 store-bought corn tortillas (or you can make your own homemade corn tortillas – see Norma's recipe on page 58)

CHICKEN TOPPING
3 tablespoons olive oil
1 medium onion, thinly sliced
2 medium tomatoes, diced
1/2 teaspoon oregano
¼ cup white vinegar
1 pound chicken breast

1 habanero pepper, grated
2 whole cloves
1 1/2 cups green cabbage, shredded

Heat approximately 1 inch of vegetable oil in a pan on high heat. Fry tortillas one at a time, until golden and crispy. Drain on paper towels.

Boil the chicken breast and onions together for 45 minutes, along with a pinch of salt, the cloves and oregano.

Once it has boiled, scoop out the chicken and onions with a slotted spoon and let them cool. Once they are cool enough to touch, shred the chicken into small pieces. Set chicken and onions aside in a bowl.

In a separate bowl, combine peppers, cabbage, tomatoes, vinegar and a pinch of salt. Place a bit of chicken and onions on top of each tortilla, and then add the cabbage-tomato mixture.

Yields 8 salbutes.

Garnachas (Tostadas with Beans)

Chef Esther, Changes in Latitudes Bed and Breakfast, San Pedro, Belize

12 tostadas (you can either use store-bought, or buy your own fresh corn tortillas and fry them yourself – see instructions below)
1 15-ounce can black beans
1 ½ cup diced onions
½ cup shredded cabbage
1 habanero pepper, finely chopped
A few tablespoons of distilled white vinegar
3 ounces grated cheese
½ teaspoon salt
Vegetable oil

Heat the beans with the liquid over low to medium heat and simmer for 5-10 minutes. Remove from heat.

Place the onions, cabbage and habaneros in a large jar or bowl, and toss with vinegar. Add a dash of salt.

If you decide to fry your own corn tortillas, place them in a warmed oven directly on a rack for just a few minutes to evaporate some water before frying (don't bake them). Layer about an inch of vegetable oil in a pan over high heat. When hot, add the tortilla, which should immediately float and bubble. Cook until golden brown, and then remove immediately so the tortillas don't burn.

Serve tortillas topped with the beans, cabbage salad and cheese.

Yields 12 garnachas.

Thanks to Chef Esther for contributing her recipe and supporting women leaders in Belize and Nicaragua.

Enchiladas (Fried Empanadas Filled with Meat and Rice)

Debora Espinoza Arce, Bluefields, Nicaragua

SHELL
8 large corn tortillas (store
  bought or homemade, see p. 58)
Vegetable oil for deep-frying

see p. 58

FILLING
1 pound of ground beef
1 cup rice
1 large onion, diced
1 bell pepper, diced
Salt and pepper to taste
1 teaspoon ground annatto seed or achiote
  paste (optional)

BATTER
3 eggs
1/2 cup flour

kitchen leader
100% of the proceeds from this book benefit the economic and professional development of women like Debora. See Debora's story, page 75.

See Debora's story, page 75.

Cook the rice according to package instructions and set aside. Sauté the peppers, onions, ground annatto and ground beef together until the meat is cooked. Combine the meat mixture and fully-cooked rice, adding a bit of salt and pepper to taste. Set aside.

In another bowl, whisk the eggs and flour together to form a batter. Set aside.

If you have a deep fryer, heat to about 375 degrees. Otherwise, a deep pot filled halfway with oil (enough to cover the enchiladas) will work fine.

Heat corn tortillas in a skillet for a minute or two, turning once. This will make the tortillas more pliable and easier to fill prior to frying. Once soft, remove the tortilla and place a spoonful of meat and rice mixture at the center of one half of the tortilla. Be careful not to overstuff. Gently fold the other half of the tortilla over the filling. Apply the egg and flour batter around the tortilla's outer edges, as if it were glue. Gently pressing with your fingers, seal the enchilada shut. It's helpful to fill all of your tortillas this way first and have them ready to fry one after another. When they are all assembled, you're ready to begin frying. Lightly cover each enchilada in batter prior to dropping it into the hot oil.

Fry enchiladas one at a time. Enchiladas are done once they float in the oil and the shell is golden brown.

Yields 8 enchiladas.

In Nicaragua, enchiladas are often served with slaw made of shredded cabbage, vinegar, and either hot sauce or finely diced habaneros or jalapeños. See Debora's cabbage slaw recipe on page 74.

Shrimp Ceviche

San Pedro, Belize

½ pound raw, cleaned shrimp, tails removed
2 cups tomatoes, diced
1 large onion, diced
½ red bell pepper, diced
12 sprigs cilantro, chopped
1 habanero pepper, minced
Juice of 5 limes
Salt to taste

Ceviche is traditionally eaten raw—the lime juice "cooks" the shrimp. However, if you prefer to cook the shrimp, you can blanch it in boiling water for 3-5 minutes, removing it as soon as it turns pink, and chop.

Rinse the cleaned shrimp in cold water. Chop the raw shrimp and place it in a bowl with lime juice to cover. Allow it to soak in the lime juice for 20-30 minutes to "cook", until shrimp is pink. Add the diced tomatoes, onions, red bell pepper, cilantro, and the habanero pepper, mixing gently. Add salt to taste.

Serves 4.

Guacamole with Hard-boiled Eggs

Doña Pinita, Owner and Chef, La Terraza Margarita Restaurant, Managua, Nicaragua

2 large avocados
4 hardboiled eggs
4 teaspoons lemon juice
¼ cup onion, diced
1 ½ teaspoon salt

Peel the avocados and cut them into small cubes. Dice the hardboiled eggs. In a large bowl, mix the avocados, eggs, onion, lemon juice and salt together with a fork, mashing the avocados until you reach the right texture. Serve immediately.

Serves 4.

Thanks to Chef Doña Pinita for contributing her recipe and supporting women leaders in Belize and Nicaragua. Read more about Doña Pinita on page 81.

Street foods in Nicaragua and Belize

In Nicaragua and Belize, fast food rarely means McDonald's or KFC. Instead, people visit roadside carts, stands, and markets where vendors dole out their specialties.

After a long day at work, Nicaraguans will often pick up a dish of fried chicken with cabbage slaw and plantain chips from their favorite stand (see p. 74). Also famous is vigorón (see p. 72), a dish of fried yucca topped with cabbage slaw and chicharrón (pork rinds).

In Belize, vendors sell homemade snacks – plantain chips (see p. 57), pepitos (roasted pumpkin seeds), and cocobrut (a candy made of chopped coconut meat and sugar). Garnachas and salbutes (see pages 28-29) are deep fried dishes made with corn tortillas and topped or stuffed with various combinations of cheese, beans, onions, meats, and spices.

Nicaraguan and Belizean street fare is satisfying, cheap, portable and varied. Vendors put unique spins on these dishes, adding a special sauce or ingredient to distinguish their product from the competition. Nicaraguan and Belizean street foods are also notable for their creative and economical use of resources; nothing edible is thrown away. Nicaraguans mix pig's blood with rice and spices to make a delicious sausage called moronga. Some might find the idea of moronga, well, blood-curdling, but it's actually quite delicious. Moronga is hearty, earthy, and richly spiced with onions, pepper, mint and chiles. In Belize, cowfoot soup is made by slow-cooking cow feet and oxtail along with allspice, okra and potatoes. It takes many hours to draw the flavors out of the bones in order to create a thick and delicious soup, but one bite tells you it's worth all the trouble.

Food seen on the street in Nicaragua, left column, top to bottom: Chicken taco, frito, moronga

Food seen on the street in Belize, right column, top to bottom: pupusas, fried conch fritters, cowfoot soup

Soups & St

ews

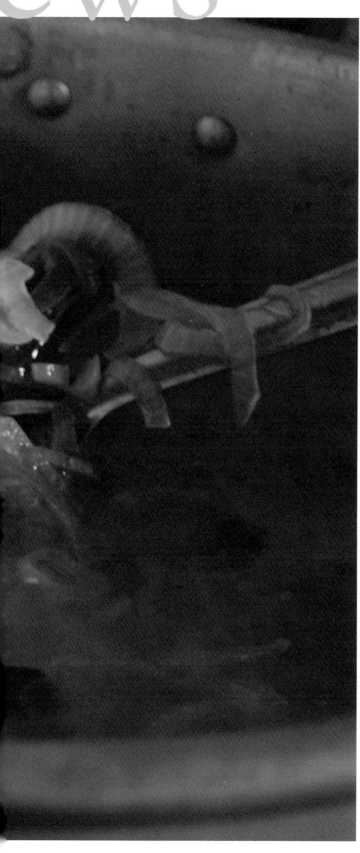

Left, clockwise:
Escabeche
(p. 46), Indio
Viejo (p. 41), and
Chimole (p. 42).

Hudut with Falumou (Garifuna Fish and Coconut Stew with Mashed Plantains)

Terese Neil, Belize City, Belize

3 14-ounce cans coconut milk

2 cups of water

2 pounds snapper or other white fish, cut into large pieces

1 onion, finely sliced

Juice of one lime

2 cloves garlic, finely chopped

4 fresh basil leaves

1 teaspoons dried thyme

4 oregano leaves, or 2 tablespoons dried oregano

1 hot pepper, diced (jalepeño or habenero)

1/2 teaspoon black pepper

1/2 teaspoon salt

Season the fish with lime juice, salt, pepper and thyme. Pour the coconut milk and water into a saucepan and heat on medium-high heat. Add garlic, onions, garlic, basil, oregano, hot peppers and black pepper and bring to a boil. Add the fish, stirring constantly to avoid curdling. Allow to simmer for 20 minutes or until fish is cooked.

Living with nine children in a two-room home, Terese works hard to make ends meet. She often picks up construction jobs when they are available and works as a cook for the local police department. Terese also travels around her neighborhood on her bike, selling homemade bread and fresh mangoes. In Belize, the cost of education can be prohibitive – even public school fees total several hundred dollars per year. Terese would love to see all of her children complete their education.

Falumou is traditionally served with hudut, a side dish of mashed green plantains. Alternatively, the dish can be eaten by itself or over hot white rice.

kitchen leader

100% of the proceeds from this book benefit the economic and professional development of women like Terese.

Above: Terese's freshly prepared falumou. Below: hudut.

Hudut (mashed plantains)

3 green plantains
1 ripe (yellow) plantain
1 teaspoon salt

Peel the plantains and boil them with salt for about 15-20 minutes, until the plantains are tender when poked with a fork. Remove them from the pot and let them cool. Mash until smooth with a potato masher, or in an electric mixer on low speed.

To eat the traditional Garifuna way, eat one bite of mashed plantains with each spoonful of soup.

Serves 8.

Sopa de Albóndigas (Chicken and Squash Stew with Meatballs)

Sofia Esperanza Salgado, Managua, Nicaragua

2 ½ pounds chicken (a whole chicken is best)
2 ½ quarts water
2 cloves of garlic, crushed
1 medium onion
1 green pepper
4 sprigs of cilantro
4 sprigs of mint
1 tablespoon paprika
1/3 cup bitter orange juice (half orange juice/half lemon juice can be substituted)
½ pound of cassava or yucca root
½ pound of quequisque (taro root is a very close relative – potato can be substituted as well)
2 pounds ripe butternut squash or pumpkin, chopped
1 cup of corn
Salt and pepper to taste

Remove the skin from chicken and cut the chicken into medium-sized pieces.

Coat each piece of chicken with half the bitter orange juice, and season with paprika and salt. Add the chicken and garlic to a pot of boiling water to cook.

Peel the cassava and quequisque, and cut them into medium slices. Cut the squash or pumpkin into medium pieces. When the chicken is cooked, add all the vegetables and continue boiling. Squeeze the juice from the remaining half of the bitter orange, and add the chopped cilantro and mint. Continue boiling. When vegetables are almost all the way cooked, add meatballs (see recipe below). Cook until vegetables and meatballs are well-cooked.

MEATBALLS (TO ADD TO THE SOUP):
1 clove garlic, crushed
1 pound chicken breast
2 cups cornmeal
½ cup water
1 teaspoon paprika
4 sprigs of mint, finely chopped
4 leaves of cilantro, finely chopped
1 small onion, finely chopped
Salt to taste

Boil the chicken breast in just enough water to cover the chicken, and add crushed garlic. When the chicken is cooked through, remove from the pot and chop finely, reserving the broth. Mix the cornmeal with the chicken broth to form a dough.

Once the consistency is dough-like, add the minced chicken, paprika, mint, cilantro, onion and salt. Knead the ingredients well and form into small balls. The balls are added to the soup while it is still boiling.

Serves 8.

Recipe adapted from Sofia Esperanza Salgado and Esperanza Pereira of Managua. Thanks to Chef Pereira for contributing her recipe and supporting women leaders in Belize and Nicaragua.

Sofia feels lucky to be alive. When she was 15, she was almost killed by a dump truck while working as a trashpicker in La Chureca – a common danger because drivers often cannot see trashpickers amid the mountains of waste. La Chureca is Central America's largest trash dump, located on the northwest side of Nicaragua's capital city, Managua.

Due to the long hours she spent working in the dump, she fell behind in math and writing and had to repeat one year of school. She also struggled because many of her high school classes required Internet research, and she didn't know how to use a computer.

She found her way to the NicaHOPE jewelry project, an initiative of the Fabretto Children's Foundation. The project trains and employs women in jewelry-making. In just a few half-days

kitchen leader
100% of the proceeds from this book benefit the economic and professional development of women like Sofia.

Sofia (left) sits with one of her students at NicaHOPE.

per week, each student earns more than she'd earn in a week at the dump. Jewelry makers work inside, sheltered from the heat, fumes and dangerous conditions. They have free time to go to school and take care of their families. Soon after Sofia began to make jewelry, she proved herself a star student and now teaches more than 60 students every week.

Fabretto also offers computer classes, and Sofia was finally able to keep up with school assignments. In 2009, Sofia became one of the first people in her community to finish high school, along with her sister Mery (see Mery's story on page 71). Sofia will take her university exam next year and hopes to study computer science.

Indio Viejo (Beef and Vegetable Stew)

Cristina Fletes, Managua, Nicaragua

MASA

6 corn tortillas
2 cups milk
2 chopped tomatoes
1 small onion, sliced
1 cup masa harina flour
1 ½ cup broth in which the meat was cooked
1 tablespoon achiote paste (paprika is a close substitute)
½ cup grated queso fresco
¼ cup mint leaves, washed
3 tablespoons butter

Masa serves as the "glue" that holds this thick stew together. While you're preparing the masa, start boiling the meat, so that the broth will be ready in time to add to the masa.

Cut the tortillas in slices and leave them in milk for three hours. In a blender, add the milk, soaked tortillas, tomatoes, onion, achiote paste, broth and mint and blend until the consistency is thick, almost like a paste.

Heat the mixture in a pan on low heat, stirring constantly. Add the masa harina flour a little at a time, then the butter and queso fresco. Continue stirring on low heat.

MEAT AND VEGETABLES

1 pound of beef (flank or skirt steak can be used, as well as brisket)
1 onion, sliced
4 tomatoes, chopped
3 red bell peppers, chopped
1/3 cup bitter orange juice (half orange juice/half lemon juice can be substituted)
¼ cup mint leaves
1/3 cup vegetable oil for frying

Boil the meat in about 2 quarts of water. When the meat is fully cooked through, remove from the pot and reserve the broth for later. Let the meat cool, then shred it.

In a separate, large frying pan, sauté the onions, tomatoes and peppers with vegetable oil until soft. Add the shredded beef. Add the masa to the beef, tomatoes, onions and peppers. Add the bitter orange juice, mint leaves, and the 2-3 cups reserved beef broth. Stir constantly and simmer until thickened.

Serves 8.

Recipe adapted from Cristina Fletes of Managua and Chef Doña Pinita of La Terraza Margarita. Thanks to Doña Pinita for contributing her recipe and supporting women leaders in Belize and Nicaragua.

kitchen leader
100% of the proceeds from this book benefit the economic and professional development of women like Cristina.

Cristina never dreamed of attending university. No one she knew from the trash dump had ever finished high school. But in 2008, when she started working at the NicaHOPE jewelry project, she began to earn enough money to support herself without having to collect cans and bottles at the dump, and was finally able to focus on her studies. She became a teacher at Fabretto's center in 2010, and her colleagues there encouraged her to prepare for the rigorous university entrance exam.

She and co-worker Mery studied every Saturday for a year, and they became the first two people from La Chureca to attend university. She is now in her second year at the University of Managua, studying special education. She is the captain of her soccer team, Las Leonas de Fabretto, and serves as the Board Secretary of the recently established NicaHOPE jewelry cooperative.

Indio Viejo is a slow-cooked, thick Nicaraguan stew. It relies heavily on local staples like corn, and is often served as the main dish.

Chimole
(Black Stew)

Mercedes*, Progresso, Belize

3 pounds chicken (approximately
   1 whole chicken, cut into pieces)
5 tablespoons black recado
2 tablespoons black pepper
½ teaspoon salt
1 medium onion, diced
2 chicken bouillon cubes
4 cloves garlic, peeled and crushed
1 tablespoon ground cloves
2 tablespoons allspice
1 tablespoon epazote (dried Mexican
   oregano; Italian oregano can be
   substituted)
1 teaspoon cumin seeds
½ pound cabbage
1 15-ounce can coconut milk
3 potatoes, diced
½ pound pumpkin or squash, diced
3 plantains, peeled and cut in half
12 cups of water
6 boiled eggs, thinly sliced lengthwise
Vegetable oil (for frying)
Optional: Corn tortillas or coconut rice

Gather your spices (crushed or minced garlic, allspice, cloves, Mexican oregano and cumin seeds). Set aside ¼ of these spices for the chicken rub, and save the other ¾ for the broth. Season the chicken with half the black recado, ¼ of your gathered spices, salt and black pepper. In a large soup pot, add a tablespoon or two of vegetable oil and heat on medium-high heat. Add the seasoned chicken and diced onions, and fry for 15-20 minutes until the chicken is golden brown.

In a separate bowl, mix 12 cups of water with the other ¾ of your reserved spices and the rest of the black recado. Add the diced potatoes and pumpkin. When the chicken is golden brown, add the water, bouillon cubes and vegetables to the pot. Add the boiled eggs. Let everything boil together for 1 hour until vegetables are soft.

Chimole can be eaten with coconut rice or with corn tortillas. To make the rice, mix 2 cups of white rice with 1/2 cup coconut milk, 1/2 cup water, and ½ teaspoon salt. Boil at medium heat for 30 minutes or until all water is absorbed.

Serves 8.

*Name changed to protect identity

kitchen leader

100% of the proceeds from this book benefit the economic and professional development of women like Mercedes*.

Mercedes, 39, is a single mother who works as a domestic worker, cooking and cleaning for a local family. After suffering years of abuse at the hands of her husband, Mercedes found the strength to leave, despite her husband's threats to harm her and her children.

Last year, Mercedes was able to safely move into a small home with her children where they are able to enjoy family meals once again. "Cooking makes me feel happy and complete, especially since it makes my children very happy and healthy," said Mercedes.

This recipe is her youngest child's favorite dish.

Chimole is a flavorful, dark-colored stew common in Belize – it's often called "black dinner." The black color comes from black recado, a traditional spice blend in Belize made from charred chiles, black pepper, annatto seeds, and other ingredients. It can be found in Latin grocery stores, well-stocked supermarkets, or ordered online.

Split Peas and Pig Tails

Yolanda Castillo, Dangriga, Belize

1 pound pig tails (cured or salted)
1 pound split peas
1 pound ham hocks
1 medium onion, diced
1 medium red pepper, diced
½ carrot, sliced (optional)
1 tablespoon salt
1 tablespoon black pepper
1 tablespoon oregano
1 stick butter
Steamed white rice, for serving

Boil the pig tails in 2 quarts water for 1 1/2 hours, changing the water every half hour until the pig tails are soft and most of the salt has been removed. Boil the split peas and ham hocks in 2 quarts water until the split peas are soft, about 1 hour. Remove the ham hocks from the pot. Add the onions, peppers and carrot (optional) to the split peas and season with the salt, black pepper and oregano. Boil until the vegetables are soft, about 20 minutes. Add the softened pig tails and the butter. Let cook for another 15 minutes until done. Serve over steamed white rice.

Thanks to Yolanda and her husband Rhodel for contributing this recipe and supporting women leaders in Belize and Nicaragua.

Yolanda Castillo was born and raised in Dangriga, Belize, and operates her own restaurant, Garifuna Flava, in Chicago.

This recipe was featured on the TV show "Diners, Drive-Ins and Dives" on the Food Network in the U.S.

Yolanda (third from left) and her husband Rhodel (far right) with their family and Food Network host Guy Fieri.

Run Down (Caribbean Soup of Meat, Coconut Milk and Vegetables)

Eva Fianca Álvarez Blandón, Bluefields, Nicaragua

2 pounds beef ribs or brisket, chopped into bite-size pieces
4 14-ounce cans of coconut milk
2 green bananas, peeled and diced
1 pound cassava or yucca, peeled and diced (pre-peeled yucca can be found in many grocers' freezer sections)
1 pound quequisque (taro root may be substituted), peeled and diced
½ of a breadfruit (2 potatoes may be substituted), peeled and diced
2 ripe plantains, peeled and diced
2 cloves garlic, minced
1 medium onion, chopped
1 medium red bell pepper, diced
1 whole chile de cabro (1 scotch bonnet or habanero pepper can be substituted)
1 chicken bouillon cube plus water or enough chicken stock to cover the meat
Salt and black pepper to taste
1 tablespoon oregano

In a large uncovered pot, bring the coconut milk to a boil and add the cassava, quequisque, onion, pepper and whole chile pepper. Add the minced garlic and herbs. Ler the pot simmer for 15-20 minutes or until the vegetables are tender.

In a separate pot, add the meat, pouring enough chicken stock over it to cover. Boil the meat until almost all the way cooked. Remove from the pot, let cool and cut into roughly bite-size pieces. Add the meat to the vegetables simmering in the pot. Add the bananas, breadfruit (if using), and plantain.

Leave the pot to simmer until the fruits are soft and the meat is fully cooked. Remove the pot from the heat and let rest for 20 minutes for the flavors to meld. Remove the chile pepper before serving.

Serves 8.

kitchen leader

Eva started her jewelry-making business a few years ago. She's completely self-taught, and started out with simple designs before progressing to more complex pieces. She works with stones, pearls, plastic and glass, and sells her jewelry to family, friends and other women in her community. As her enterprise grows, she plans to buy a bigger work table and a book of jewelry patterns with exact measurements, in order to use her materials more efficiently and streamline production.

Eva hopes her entrepreneurship will inspire her two daughters. "As mothers, we're examples for our children as women," she said. "I want to teach them to keep studying and to move forward. I also want to be an example for other women, that we can make it on our own."

Run Down is typically served in Bluefields in the month of May when all the plants and trees are blooming.

Eva Fianca Álvarez Blandón (right) with her neighbor and good friend Nancy Bermudez Notis (left) on the front porch of Nancy's home. See Nancy's recipe p. 86.

Escabeche (Spicy Stew with Chicken and Onions)

Brenda Sedassie, Progresso, Belize

3 pounds chicken, cut into large
   pieces (using a whole chicken so as
   to include a mix of white and dark
   meat is best)
8 whole allspice seeds
1 tablespoon dried oregano
6 whole cloves
1 teaspoon cumin seeds
1 teaspoon black pepper
1 chicken bouillon cube
4-5 cloves of garlic
6 large white onions, thinly sliced
   into rings
1 cup white vinegar
2 whole jalapeño peppers
Salt and pepper to taste
Vegetable oil for frying

Fresh corn tortillas to serve on the
   side (optional)

Place the chicken in a large soup
pot, and fill about halfway with water
(enough to fully cover the chicken). Add
all the spices except vinegar, onions
and jalapeños, and begin boiling. Once
boiling has begun, lower the heat so the
chicken soup simmers gently. Let cook
for 45 minutes.

While the chicken is cooking, boil
another saucepan of water. Place the
sliced onions into the pot and reduce
heat to medium. Let the onions cook for
30 minutes or so.

Once the chicken is fully cooked,

place in a bowl to season before
grilling, reserving the chicken broth.
Drain the onions and add them to the
chicken broth. Add vinegar little by
little (more can be used for a stronger
taste, some can be replaced with water
if you find the broth too sour). Add the
jalapeño peppers, and allow the broth to
cook another 15 to 30 minutes.

While broth simmers, rub the boiled
chicken with salt and pepper, and fry it
in a pan with vegetable oil until the skin
turns golden brown. Serve each bowl of
escabeche with a piece of chicken. Corn
tortillas are traditionally served with
escabeche as a side accompaniment.

Serves 8.

Brenda used to operate a small grocery store out of her home, selling basic goods like flour, sugar and milk. She was generous and allowed many friends and neighbors to buy items on credit when money was short.

Eventually, after too many people put their purchases on a tab, Brenda had to close her store. Since then, she's learned more about operating a small business. Brenda hopes to open up her grocery store again and increase her inventory so that she can make a profit.

"I want to be able to sustain my family, send my kids to get an education, and be a role model for other single mothers," she said. Escabeche is her children's favorite recipe.

Salads & Si

des

Left, clockwise:
Dried beans for
sale in an open-air
market in Belize
City, fruit for sale
in Belize City, and
homemade flour
tortillas topped
with taco fixings
(p. 58).

Pilau Rice

Brenda Cutkelvin, Belize City, Belize

1 pound chicken breast (shrimp can be substituted)

2 teaspoons complete seasoning, divided (if this isn't available, a few shakes each of black pepper, salt, onion powder, garlic powder and oregano can be substituted)

1 ½ teaspoons dried chicken stock

¼ cup sugar

1 quart chicken or vegetable broth

¼ cup vegetable oil

½ cup carrots, finely chopped

½ cup corn

½ cup peas

1 medium onion, chopped

1 medium sweet pepper, chopped

½ teaspoon dried thyme

2 cups rice

2 tablespoons powdered coconut milk

Salt and pepper to taste

Fried plantains for garnish (optional)

Dice the chicken into 1-inch cubes. Season with pepper, 1 teaspoon complete seasoning, thyme, and dried chicken stock. Let marinate in a plastic bag or bowl for one hour. In skillet on high heat, add the vegetable oil and sugar and cook until the sugar burns. Add chicken to skillet, and cook a few minutes on each side, turning so the chicken gets coated with burnt sugar. Add broth and bring to a boil, cooking for 20 minutes. Add the rice and vegetables, 1 teaspoon complete seasoning, and the powdered coconut milk. Liquid should be about half an inch over rice. Lower heat and let the rice simmer until all liquid is absorbed. Serve immediately.

Serves 4-5.

Brenda's family keeps her very busy – she's a mother of 5 children and grandmother of 7. When she's not taking care of her family, she helps lead her neighborhood's community sewing cooperative.

Started by her friend and neighbor Indira Bartley, the cooperative enables members to share a sewing machine and pool their resources to buy thread and fabric. They sew school uniforms and complete other projects to generate income. Brenda is an expert seamstress and serves as the head teacher for the sewing program. She helps train other women in her community, offering them a chance to participate and earn income for their own families.

kitchen leader

100% of the proceeds from this book benefit the economic and professional development of women like Brenda.

Potato and Egg Salad

Katty Vasquez Nicaragua, San Isidro, Nicaragua

1 pound potatoes, peeled and diced
½ carrot, peeled and chopped into small pieces
½ an onion, chopped into small pieces
1 medium tomato, diced
1 cup mayonnaise
1-2 hardboiled eggs, depending on your taste
Salt and pepper

Boil the potatoes and carrots until cooked, then drain water and set aside.

Boil the eggs and let them cool before dicing into small pieces. In a large bowl, mix the potatoes, carrots, eggs, tomatoes and onions together and add the mayonnaise. Add salt and pepper to taste. Mix well and chill in refrigerator for 4 hours before serving.

Serves 4.

Thanks to Katty for contributing her recipe and supporting women leaders in Belize and Nicaragua. Read more about Katty on p. 17.

Gertrude is an enterprising woman devoted to her community. She remains very involved in the local Garifuna church, and often spends her free time organizing discussions with the young men living in her neighborhood about the dangers of gang involvement. She works three days a week for the Human Development Department inspecting homes.

Gertrude has shared a recipe for a Belizean favorite, Darasa. Loosely translated, Darasa means "slow" in Garifuna, so leave plenty of time to try your hand at this dish!

kitchen leader

100% of the proceeds from this book benefit the economic and professional development of women like Gertrude.

Darasa (Garifuna Banana and Coconut Dumplings)

Gertrude Martinez, Belize City, Belize

6 green bananas (unripe)
1 teaspoon garlic salt
1 small onion, diced
2 teaspoons black pepper
1/2 cup coconut milk
Banana leaves if you can find them, otherwise corn husks or aluminum foil, cut into 8-inch x 8-inch squares

Peel and grate bananas. Mix grated bananas with coconut milk, and season with black pepper and salt. Drop about 5-6 tablespoons of the mixture into each clean banana leaf or piece of foil.

Fold and tie leaves into rectangular shapes, or fold over foil and seal. Place them into a large pan and cover with water. Boil for about 1 hour. When water is cooled, take the darasas out and let them cool down. Serve warm.

Serves 6-8.

Darasa is a side dish often eaten with meat or fish. However, these sweet coconut and banana dumplings are delicious on their own.

Maduros en Gloria (Sweet Baked Plantains)

Verónica Cuadra Miranda, Bluefields, Nicaragua

5 ripe plantains
½ stick butter, softened
1/3 cup of sugar
½ pound queso blanco, grated (any fresh,
   white cheese can be substituted)
Ground cinnamon to taste

Peel the plantains and slice them in half down the middle. Place them in a greased baking pan. Cover plantains with butter, sugar, and grated cheese, and top with the cinnamon. Bake in the oven at 350 degrees for 25-30 minutes.

Serves 6.

kitchen leader

100% of the proceeds from this book benefit the economic and professional development of women like Verónica.

Verónica works as a secretary in a center for abused women in Bluefields, Nicaragua, and she supplements her income with her own enterprise, making hand-painted banners and signs for local organizations and churches.

Both she and her husband are talented artists, and have decorated their home with their own paintings. Verónica has also taught art classes out of her home to local youth. She enjoys working with children in order to develop their creativity.

Maduros en Gloria is Verónica's favorite dish, and is a typical side to her family's lunches.

Picking the perfect plantain

Many Belizean and Nicaraguan recipes call for plantains, the larger cousins of the banana that can be found in Latin American or Caribbean supermarkets. Unlike most fruits, plantains can be enjoyed at various stages of ripeness: green, yellow, or black.

Green, unripe plantains (verdes in Spanish) have a firmer texture and low sugar content, and taste more like a starchy vegetable than a fruit. They can be boiled or fried for dishes like hudut (see p. 39) and fried plantain chips. As a snack or side, fried plantains are delicious with a little salt and your favorite salsa or hot sauce. Wash them down with a cold Toña or Belikin beer.

Plantains are ripe when they turn yellow, and it's normal for a ripe plantain to have some brown spots. In fact, plantains are edible even when they're almost completely black. The darker the fruit, the sweeter it will be, so purchase your plantains according to how sweet or savory your recipe is. Ripe plantains are called maduros in Spanish, and are much softer than green plantains. Typically fried or baked, ripe plantains' high sugar content makes them ideal ingredients in sweet dishes like maduros en gloria (see p. 54) or milkshakes.

Ripe plantains aren't always available in U.S. grocery stores. If you have to buy green plantains, simply place them in a paper bag and let them ripen them for a few days on your countertop. Avoid plantains that are squishy or those with peels beginning to dry out.

Crispy Fried Plantain Chips

Indira Bartley, Belize City, Belize

3 green plantains
Approximately 4 cups vegetable oil for frying

Peel then slice plantains very thin, about 1/8-inch or thinner. A mandoline for slicing works very well; otherwise a knife will do. Pour vegetable oil into large cooking pot and heat on medium-high. Add the plantains when the oil is at a low boil. Chips are ready when lightly browned. Remove plantains and drain. These chips are a great snack and pair well with a side or dip of your choice.

kitchen leader

100% of the proceeds from this book benefit the economic and professional development of women like Indira.

Indira Bartley founded the Regina Martinez Foundation in memory of her mother, a well-known and respected community leader in Belize. Regina started the arts and crafts market in Belize City in order to help rural Mayan women earn income from selling their handiwork. She also started the Belizean Rural Women's Association in order to help women gain economic power through farming. She led a campaign to distribute condoms to help prevent the spread of STIs even though doing so was controversial.

The Regina Martinez Foundation works to improve the lives of women in the Jane Usher Boulevard area, which currently suffers from some of the highest crime rates in Belize City. Members have organized to lobby for additional park space for children, as the only park in the neighborhood is a dilapidated square of concrete. They are also advocating for funding for indoor plumbing, which many neighborhood families lack, and the installation of street lights to deter crime and gang violence.

The Regina Martinez Foundation has developed a sewing course to teach members marketable job skills. Currently two of the graduates are supporting themselves through their sewing work. More would be able to do so if they could afford additional sewing machines.

Photo, above: Indira (right) with her mentor, Cynthia Pitts (left).
Photo, left: Indira's freshly fried plantain chips.

Crunchy Corn Tortillas

Norma Ondina Soliz, Progresso, Belize

TORTILLAS
2 cups masa harina (finely ground
  corn flour)
1/4 cup white flour
1 teaspoon salt
1/2 teaspoon baking powder
3/4 cup water
Vegetable oil for frying

Mix together the masa harina, flour, salt and baking powder. Add the water, mixing well, using just enough to make a stiff dough (if the dough is too thin or too dry, add more masa harina or water as needed). Let the dough sit for 5 minutes. Pinch off pieces of dough to make 1-inch balls. Flatten them into tortillas about 4 inches in diameter. Heat approximately 1 inch of vegetable oil in a pan on high heat. Fry tortillas one at a time until golden and crispy. Drain on paper towels.

Makes approximately 10 tortillas.

kitchen leader

100% of the proceeds from this book benefit the economic and professional development of women like Norma. See Norma's story, page 28.

Flour Tortillas

Daisy Magaña, Progresso, Belize

5 cups flour
2 teaspoons salt
4 teaspoons baking powder
1 ½ cups water
3 tablespoons of shortening or
  vegetable oil

Mix flour, baking powder and salt together. Add the shortening/vegetable oil into the middle of the mixture. Add water a little at a time and knead until smooth (about 4-5 minutes.) Divide the dough into about 15 balls, brush some shortening/oil on top of them and let the dough rest for 5 minutes. Roll each dough ball on a floured surface until they are very flat.

Preheat an ungreased frying pan to medium heat. Cook each tortilla for about 1 minute on each side.

Makes 15 tortillas.

Thanks to Daisy Magaña for contributing her recipe and supporting women leaders in Belize and Nicaragua.

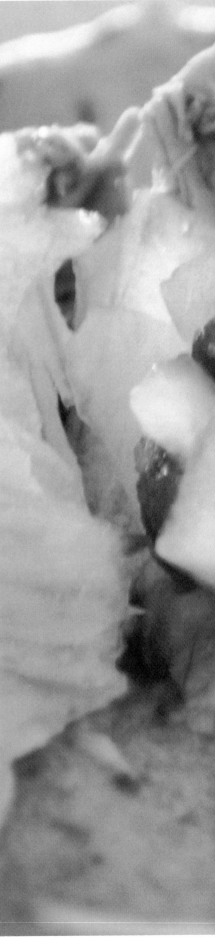

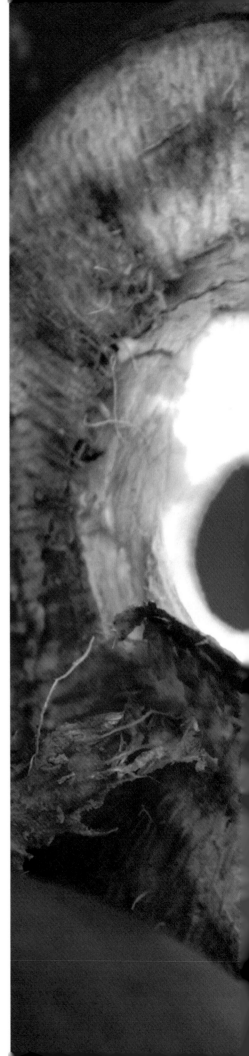

Coconut Rice and Beans

Chef Dulce Maria Durán, Laguna Grill, Progresso, Belize

2/3 cup dried red kidney beans
or black beans, rinsed and
picked over
1 cup coconut milk
1 medium onion, chopped
2 cups uncooked rice, cleaned
and rinsed
¼ cup coconut oil or vegetable
shortening
1 teaspoon salt
Water

45-60 minutes or until soft.

Add the coconut milk, onions, rice,
oil, and salt into a pot large enough to
allow contents to double in size. Add
water to cover about ¼ inch above
the ingredients. Cover, and bring to a
boil. After most of the liquid has been
absorbed, stir and reduce heat to very
low. Let simmer for about 15 more
minutes, or until the rice is soft.

Serves 4.

Soak the beans in 3-4 cups of water in a
large pot for 4-6 hours before cooking.
Do not drain. Bring the beans to a boil
(in their soaking broth) and simmer for

Thanks to Chef Dulce Maria Durán of the Laguna
Grill in Progresso, Belize, for contributing her recipe
and supporting women leaders in Belize and
Nicaragua.

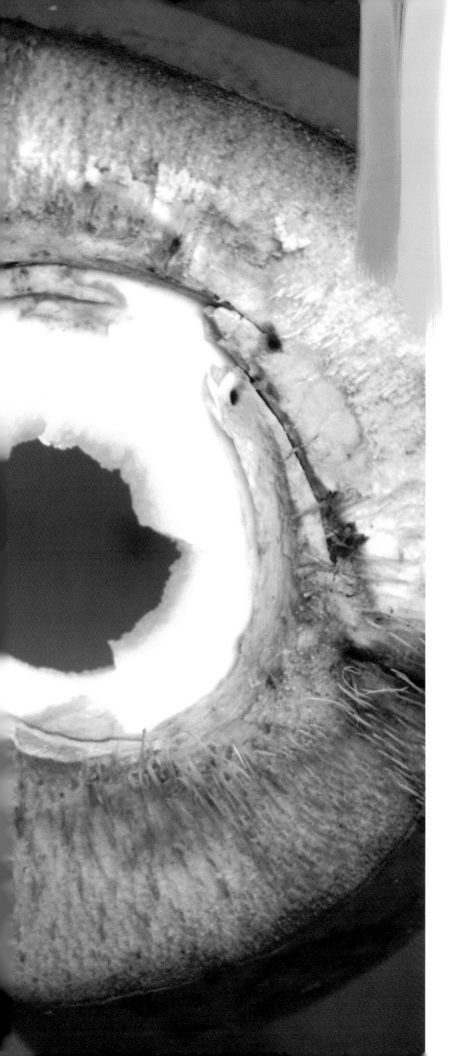

Get cracking on that coconut

Many of our recipes call for coconut milk. Of course, you make these recipes using coconut milk from the can, but the best milk is made from scratch using fresh coconut meat. Bonus—if you open up the fruit yourself, you can drink the refreshing coconut water first. Assuming you don't know how to wield a machete (often the instrument of choice for cracking open a coconut in Belize and Nicaragua), here's a beginner's guide to the coconut.

First, pick the right kind of coconut. Choose ripe, brown coconuts rather than the green ones. You can tell if a coconut is ripe by shaking it gently. If you can hear coconut water splashing around inside, then the coconut is ripe. Each coconut should yield about two cups of milk.

Next, locate the eyes of the coconut. These are the brown, bald spots on the end of the coconut and are the weakest part of the shell. Pierce the eyes with a sharp knife or a hammer and nail, and then drain the coconut water into a mixing bowl. If the water doesn't drain easily, then use the hammer and nail to make another hole on the opposite end. Save the coconut water—it's filled with healthy electrolytes!

Next, cover the coconuts completely with a kitchen towel, and split them open by smashing them with a hammer or rolling pin. Once the coconut is open, detach the coconut meat from its husk using a sharp paring knife, removing any remaining brown bits of skin from the coconut meat. Once the meat is separated from the husk, place it into the blender and add 3-4 cups hot water. Blend the mixture until smooth. Strain the coconut mixture through a cheesecloth, squeezing out as much liquid as possible. Reserve the dehydrated coconut meat in the refrigerator or freezer to use in another recipe that calls for dried coconut.

DID YOU KNOW?

In Central America, not a single part of the coconut goes to waste. The husks are used in various arts and crafts and as kindling to start a fire. The coconut water is a prized beverage, renowned for its hydrating properties. The fresh meat is grated for use in baked goods or to prepare coconut milk. The dried grated meat that remains after making coconut milk goes into a variety of desserts—coconut pie, fudge, and ice cream are just a few. The coconut is rich in trace minerals such as manganese, copper, and selenium, which are essential to the body's metabolism, immune system, and thyroid function, respectively. Coconut is also high in lauric acid, known for its antimicrobial properties.

Dinners

Left, clockwise:
Tamales steaming
(p. 67), spicy
cabbage relish (p.
69), Baked Curry
Chicken (p. 73)

Caballo Bayo:
a traditional Nicaraguan feast

Caballo Bayo is a traditional Nicaraguan feast, composed of the best Nicaraguan cooking from the Pacific coast. Preparing the spread is quite labor-intensive, since the menu often entails more than a dozen different dishes. For this reason, it's usually reserved for special occasions.

Caballo Bayo typically includes shredded beef and chicken, annatto-marinated pork ribs, chicharrón (pork rinds), moronga (blood sausage), fried beef tacos, sliced tamales pisque (pork tamales), corn tortillas (see p. 58), indio viejo (a stew of corn masa and shredded beef, see p. 41), guacamole (see p. 33), gallo pinto (see p. 16), chunks of fried and fresh cheese, cabbage salad (see p. 74), and red and green salsas.

Each dish is placed on a table in separate bowls and guests serve themselves buffet-style.

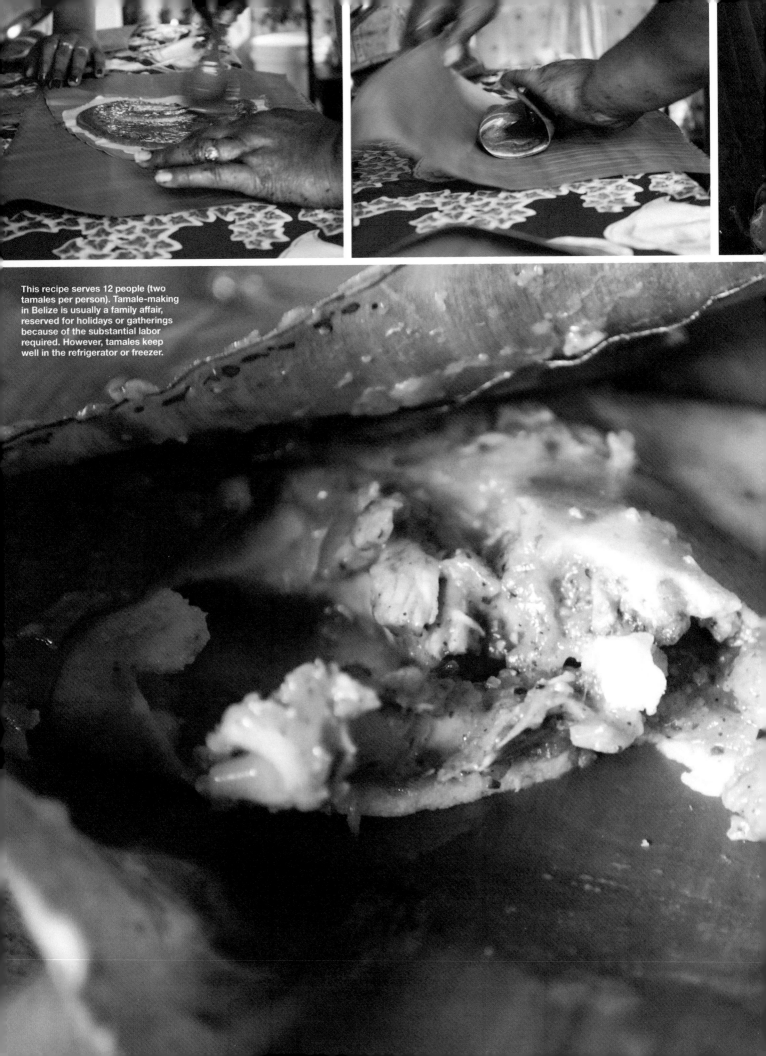

This recipe serves 12 people (two tamales per person). Tamale-making in Belize is usually a family affair, reserved for holidays or gatherings because of the substantial labor required. However, tamales keep well in the refrigerator or freezer.

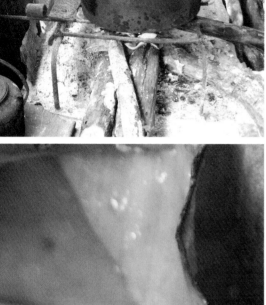

Spicy Chicken Tamales Wrapped in Banana Leaves

Lilia Ack, Progresso, Belize

3 packages plantain leaves (if you can't find plantain leaves, aluminum foil cut into 8-inch x 8 inch squares will work)

Butcher string

1 whole chicken, approximately 4 lbs (white meat only can be used if you prefer, but the traditional and more delicious way is to use meat from a whole chicken, including thighs, wings, etc.)

4 pounds masa harina

½ cup red recado (traditional Belizean spice blend – see recipe p. 68)

2 sliced onions

3 sliced tomatoes

1 cup vegetable oil

1 ½ tablespoons black pepper

6 teaspoons of salt

PREPARING THE CHICKEN

Cut the chicken into large pieces (you will place one or two pieces in each tamale). Rub the chicken with the red recado, salt, and 1 teaspoon of black pepper. Boil the chicken for an hour in 2-3 quarts of water (enough to cover the chicken). Take out the chicken when fully cooked and place in a large bowl. Save the water.

PREPARING THE DOUGH

Add 4 teaspoons of salt and 1 cup of vegetable oil to 2 ½ pounds of masa harina (reserve the other 1 ½ pound), and knead together until soft. The dough will make approximately 20-25 medium balls, each about 3 inches wide. Take each ball and flatten until the dough is thin.

PREPARING THE COL

The water used to boil the chicken is used to prepare the col, a delicious sauce that doubles as "glue" to hold the tamales together. Dilute the reserved 1 ½ pounds of masa harina in 4 cups of water and add it to the water used to boil the chicken. Stir for 30 minutes until liquid is thick.

PREPARING THE TAMALES

When all the dough is flattened, place one piece at a time on top of one plantain leaf. Spread a little col across the flattened dough. Place a piece or two of chicken, a slice of tomato and onion in the middle. Fold the dough over to seal. Wrap the plantain leaf around the tamale and fold tightly like a package. Tie butcher string around the tamale so it doesn't open up. Layer a few banana leaves on the bottom of a large cooking pot, which will keep the tamales from sticking.

When all the tamales are made and wrapped, stack them in the pot. Add just enough water to cover the top of the tamales and layer extra leaves on top. Let the pot boil for 1 hour to steam the tamales.

kitchen leader

100% of the proceeds from this book benefit the economic and professional development of women like Lilia.

Lilia and her two daughters are involved in the Progresso 4-H club, which runs after-school activities and field trips for youth. Lilia volunteers for 4-H, doing what she does best: making the best tamales in town.

Tamale sales have raised funds to clean up the Progresso lagoon and to provide school supplies to 35 kids in the club. Income from Lilia's tamales has also enabled her daughters to attend cosmetology classes, and they hope to start a family business putting their new skills to work. Lilia has made hundreds of tamales to raise money for 4-H. She and other 4-H moms often start at night and finish at dawn, in time to sell fresh, hot tamales for breakfast.

Red Recado Spice Blend

Recado is an ubiquitous spice blend across Belize. It's difficult to find outside the region, but you can make your own. Make plenty – recado can be kept in an airtight container in your refrigerator and will last several months. It can be used as a marinade or rub for chicken, beef or fish.

2 tablespoons annatto or achiote
  seeds
5 whole cloves
1 teaspoon cumin seeds
1 tablespoon dried Mexican oregano
1 tablespoon black peppercorns
2 teaspoons coarse salt
6 cloves garlic
1 teaspoon ancho chili powder
½ teaspoon cinnamon
½ teaspoon nutmeg
2 tablespoons cider vinegar
1 tablespoon bitter orange juice
  (if unavailable, substitute 1 part
  lime juice, 1 part orange juice)

Using an electric grinder or mortar and pestle, grind any whole seeds or herbs first – annatto or achiote, cloves, cumin, oregano, and peppercorns. Then, add the rest of the dry ground spices (allspice, salt, chili powder, cinnamon and nutmeg). Alternatively, ground spices can be substituted for any whole ones. Finely chop the garlic and crush into a paste. Mix the spices with the crushed garlic, and then add the vinegar and orange juice a little at a time until the mixture forms a paste about the texture of wet sand. Roll the mixture into little balls, about the size of half an egg each, and place them in an airtight container or in individual plastic bags. They will dry and harden in a day or two, and you can break off the amount you need when cooking. Red recado will keep for several months in the refrigerator (or indefinitely in the freezer) until ready to use.

In Nicaragua, carne asada is often served with gallo pinto (see p. 16), cabbage slaw (see p. 74), and fried plantains (see p. 57).

kitchen leader

100% of the proceeds from this book benefit the economic and professional development of women like Veronica. See Veronica's story, page 54.

Carne Asada

Verónica Cuadra Miranda, Bluefields, Nicaragua

2 pounds flank steak
4 green onions, sliced
½ white onion, sliced
1 red pepper, chopped
4 cloves garlic, chopped
3 ounces white vinegar
½ teaspoon pepper
1 teaspoon mustard powder
2 tablespoons Worcestershire sauce
Salt to taste

In a food processor or blender, blend all the ingredients (except the meat) to make the marinade. Marinate the meat in this sauce for several hours in the refrigerator (overnight is best).

Remove meat from the marinade and grill or barbeque until brown.

For best results, sear on high heat for 4-5 minutes on each side depending on thickness of steak.

Serves 8.

Marie Sharp's Hot Sauce (left); homemade cabbage and habanero relish (above).

Add a kick to your meals, the Belizean way

MARIE SHARP'S HOT SAUCE
(pictured left)

Marie Sharp's hot sauces are practically Belize's national condiment. In 1980, Marie Sharp began experimenting with sauces in her kitchen, using vegetables she grew in her garden. Her friends and neighbors loved them so much that she decided to start her own business. Now, Marie Sharp has a factory in Dangriga, Belize, with more than 20 employees.

Most of her sauces are carrot- and habanero-based, and heat level ranges from mild to insanely hot, with names like "No Wimps Allowed," "Belizean Heat" and the ever-ominous "Beware."

TO MAKE YOUR OWN SPICY CABBAGE RELISH:

Dice cabbage, onion, and habaneros. Add salt and pepper and toss with white vinegar to taste.

Stew Chicken

2 pounds chicken
2 tablespoons red recado (traditional
   spice blend - see recipe, p. 68)
1 cup white vinegar
1 1/2 cup Worcestershire sauce
1 tablespoon thyme
1 tablespoon cumin
1 tablespoon black pepper
2 tablespoons minced garlic
1 onion, chopped
1 habanero pepper, diced, or 1
   tablespoon red pepper flakes or hot
   sauce (optional)
Vegetable oil for frying
3-4 cups water
Salt to taste

In a bowl, mix the vinegar, Worcestershire sauce, recado and all the spices except garlic. Add chicken to the bowl and rub thoroughly with the mixture to season.

In a large frying pan, sauté the chicken on medium to high heat to brown each side. Make sure to save the marinade. When browned, add the garlic and onions and sauté together until soft, about 5 minutes. Add the chicken marinade and the water. The liquid should almost cover the chicken. If more is needed, add Worcestershire sauce a little at a time.

Cover and let simmer for about 30 minutes to cook the chicken all the way through. Add salt to taste.

Serves 4-6.

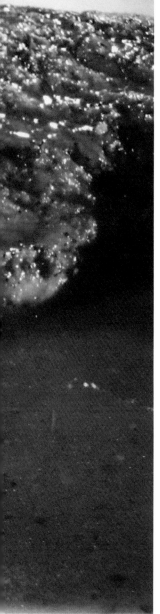

Mery (far right) works with fellow NicaHOPE teachers Sofia, center, and Cristina, left.

Arroz a la Valenciana (Rice with Chicken and Vegetables)

Mery María Moncado Salgado, Managua, Nicaragua

1 ½ cup rice
1 chicken breast
½ a carrot, finely chopped
1 green bell pepper, finely chopped
1 stalk celery, finely chopped
½ an onion, finely chopped
1 clove of garlic, minced
2 whole peeled tomatoes (canned is fine)
½ teaspoon white vinegar
1-2 tablespoons vegetable oil
1-2 tablespoons olive oil
2 cups water
2 sprigs of parsley
Salt and pepper to taste

Boil the chicken breast in 2 cups water. Add garlic and tomatoes. Boil the chicken until cooked through. When the chicken is done, remove from the broth and let cool. Save the broth and mince chicken into small pieces. Cook the rice separately according to instructions. Set aside when cooked. In a separate, large saucepan, add the vegetable oil, carrot and cooked rice. Fry the mixture until carrots are soft. Add the chicken broth. Cover the pan and let simmer until all the liquid is absorbed.

In a separate pan, sauté the onion, bell pepper, and celery. Then, add the chicken breast and sauté for a few minutes more. Finally, add the rice to the chicken, and sauté everything together until evenly cooked and there is no more liquid. Sprinkle finely chopped parsley on top.

Serves 4.

Mery used to live and work in La Chureca, collecting recyclables in the heat for less than $3 a day. But despite the difficult conditions, she was determined to finish school, and in 2009, she graduated high school with her sister Sofia — the first two students from La Chureca to do so.

A few years ago, Mery discovered NicaHOPE, a small jewelry project located at Fabretto's education center outside of La Chureca (see p. 98). She excelled at the craft, and began to teach other students until finally hired as a full-time staff member. She's currently in her second year at the University of Managua. Mery and her co-teacher Cristina Fletes (see Cristina's story on p. 41) were the first two people from La Chureca to attend university. Only 20% of students even pass the entry exam. Mery is studying Special Education Pedagogy.

It's a point of pride in the community that these women have finished school, and other children look up to them and ask them for tutoring help. "I never thought I would get here," Mery said. "I feel a great responsibility to set a good example for the other girls from La Chureca." She also coaches a youth soccer team. Her next goal is to learn English.

Vigorón (Fried Yucca Topped with Fried Pork Rind and Cabbage Slaw)

Teresa Garcia Flores, San Isidro, Nicaragua

2 ½ pounds fresh or frozen yucca
root
½ pound fried pork rinds,
crumbled (also known as
chicharrón in Nicaragua)
½ a head of red or green cabbage,
shredded
½ an onion, finely diced
½ a carrot, shredded
1 tomato, finely diced and seeded
1 beet, finely diced
½ cup white vinegar
Salt to taste

YUCCA

Peel the yucca (if using fresh – frozen will come already peeled). Cut each yucca lengthwise into 2 or 3 pieces. Boil the yucca until soft (about 15-30 minutes, depending if it's fresh or frozen). When it's about the texture of a boiled potato, it's done. Let cool, and then slice the yucca into pieces about the size and shape of small patties. Sauté with oil on medium to high heat until slightly crispy on the outside. Serve the cooked yucca on a plate and top with the pork rinds or chicharrón. Finally, top with the chilled cabbage slaw (recipe below).

CABBAGE SLAW

Sauté the beets and carrots until soft. When done, add to the raw cabbage, onions and tomatoes. Toss everything together with the white vinegar and salt to taste. Refrigerate.

Serves 4-6.

Thanks to Teresa for sharing her recipe and supporting women leaders in Belize and Nicaragua. Read more about Teresa on p. 17.

Baked Curry Chicken

Teresita Catzim, Progresso, Belize

1 whole chicken, cut into large
  pieces
4 tablespoons curry powder
3 tablespoons dried chicken stock
2 sweet peppers, chopped
2 onions, chopped
1 tablespoon black pepper
1 tablespoon butter
I cup water

Season chicken with curry, dried chicken stock and black pepper. Coat a glass baking dish with butter and place chicken in the pan. Add the water, onions and sweet pepper. Bake for an hour at 375 degrees.

Serves 4.

Thanks to Teresita for contributing her recipe and supporting women leaders in Belize and Nicaragua.

Grilled Garlic-Lime Snapper

Chef Dulce María Durán, Laguna Grill, Progresso, Belize

4 snapper fillets (any white fish can
  be used – halibut, grouper, etc.)
2 teaspoons minced garlic, blended
  with 1 teaspoon coconut or olive oil
Juice of 1 lime
1 medium onion, sliced
Salt and pepper to taste
Slice of lime for garnish

Rub fish fillet with garlic-oil mixture on both sides. Squeeze lime juice on both sides, and place fish into a sealed container and allow to marinate for at least an hour (overnight is best). Heat grill to about 400 degrees. Place fish on grill and sprinkle with salt and black pepper to taste. Cook for about 3 minutes on each side. Add onion slices to grill, and cook for a minute or two, just enough to char them a bit. Serve fish with onion slices on top and garnish with lime slice. Best served with a side of vegetables, coconut rice and beans (see p. 60) or a garden salad.

Serves 4.

Thanks to Chef Dulce María Durán for contributing this recipe and supporting women leaders in Belize and Nicaragua.

Frito (Fried Chicken atop Tangy Cabbage Slaw and Plantain Chips)

Debora Espinoza Arce, Bluefields, Nicaragua

CHICKEN

1 pound chicken legs
3-4 cups milk (enough to cover the chicken in the marinade)
1 stick melted butter
3 cloves garlic, peeled
4 eggs
3-4 cups flour
1 tablespoon cumin
1 tablespoon paprika
1 tablespoon black pepper
1 tablespoon garlic salt
1 teaspoon salt
1 teaspoon black pepper
Vegetable oil for frying

Wash the chicken in water and pat dry. Put the chicken in a bowl and pour in the milk and melted butter. Add three whole cloves of garlic. Mix with your hands a bit. Then, cover the bowl with plastic wrap and let the chicken marinate in the refrigerator overnight.

Preheat the oven to 400 degrees. Remove the chicken and lay on a plate. In a shallow bowl or dish, mix the flour with the paprika, cumin, black pepper, salt, and garlic salt. Beat the eggs in a separate bowl. Roll each piece of chicken in the eggs, then the flour. Now, you're ready to fry. Add the oil to a pan (enough to fully cover the chicken) and fry the chicken on high heat, covered, for 8 minutes. Remove when crispy. Note: The chicken will still be undercooked on the inside. To avoid overfrying the crispy outside, bake the chicken at 400 for 10 minutes to fully cook through.

CABBAGE SLAW

1/2 a head of green cabbage, shredded
2 carrots, peeled and grated
2 medium tomatoes, diced and seeded
1 medium onion, finely chopped
1 teaspoon mustard powder
White vinegar (start with a half cup and add more as needed)
Juice of one lime

Toss the cabbage with tomatoes, onions, carrots and vinegar. Add the vinegar, mustard, lime juice and salt and pepper to taste.

FRIED PLANTAIN CHIPS—SEE P. 57.

Serves 4.

Debora is a survivor of domestic violence. She found the strength to escape when she realized she didn't want to expose her children to violence.

Debora supports herself and her children by operating a small cooking business from home. Her specialties include Nicaraguan-style ground beef enchiladas, tamales, and frito, a typical local dish of fried chicken and spicy cabbage slaw served atop fried plantains. Debora wishes to serve as an example for her children, showing them that women can run a successful business.

In her spare time, she provides volunteer support for other women who are trying to emerge from domestic violence situations.

rinks

Left, clockwise:
Pio Quinto (p. 90),
Macúa de Nicaragua
(p. 89), Pudín de
Camote (p. 78)

Pudín de Camote
(Sweet Potato Pudding)

Julia*, Progresso, Belize

4 pounds sweet potato (approximately 8
   medium-sized sweet potatoes)
1 stick butter
1 14-ounce can coconut milk
2 tablespoons vanilla extract
2-3 tablespoons ground nutmeg
3 ½ cups sugar
Optional: 1 layer of plantain leaves or banana
   leaves

Grating is the traditional way to prepare this pudding.
However, it is time-consuming and difficult labor!
Another option is to boil the sweet potatoes until
soft enough to blend in a food processor. Only blend
them for a 15-20 seconds at a time, so you can
approximate the same texture as grated potatoes –
don't puree them. The texture of the final product will
be slightly different, but the taste will be the same.

If grating by hand, wash and peel the sweet potatoes,
then grate them finely into a bowl.

After the potatoes are grated (or blended), add the
coconut milk, sugar, butter, vanilla and nutmeg. If
you're using a food processor or blender, all these
ingredients can be blended together as well. Pour into
a greased baking pan. Optional: if you have plantain
leaves, layer them on the bottom of the baking pan
and brush butter over them before pouring in the
pudding batter. Bake for 1½ hours at 350 degrees.

Serves 10-12.

*Name changed to protect identity.

Julia* immigrated to Belize in
the 1980s when civil war broke
out in her home country. She
has eight children, and the two
oldest children work to support
the family so that the younger
children can remain in school.

kitchen
leader
100% of the proceeds
from this book benefit
the economic and
professional development
of women like Julia.

Her children participate in the
Progresso 4-H club and use their
knowledge to help the family grow vegetables and
raise chickens in the backyard. Next, they plan to
add a couple of pigs to their mini-farm, for which they
have already constructed a pigpen.

"Being in the kitchen and preparing food for the
ones I love is the most rewarding feeling," Julia said.
"I wanted to share my recipe of my kids' favorite
pudding, made from the potatoes we grow in our
backyard."

Horchata (Sweet Rice Milk Drink)

Debora Espinosa Arce, Bluefields, Nicaragua

2 cups rice, cleaned and rinsed
1 teaspoon cinnamon
½ teaspoon ground cloves
1 teaspoon cocoa
½ cup sugar
3 cups milk
3 cups water
1 teaspoon vanilla
1 teaspoon ground jícaro
  seed (optional if available)

Combine the cleaned raw rice with 3 cups water in a bowl, and let it soften for 2-3 hours. Place the rice and water in a blender and blend till smooth. Strain the liquid through a strainer to remove any hard pieces that remain. Then, blend the liquid for 30 seconds with the cinnamon, sugar, cocoa, vanilla, milk, cloves and jícaro seeds and liquify until thick. Pour over ice to serve.

Serves 4.

kitchen leader
100% of the proceeds from this book benefit the economic and professional development of women like Debora. See Debora's story, page 75.

Doña Pinita at her restaurant in Managua.

Fresco de Cacao (Chocolate Rice Milk Drink)

Doña Pinita, Owner and Chef, La Terraza
Margarita Restaurant, Nicaragua, Managua

2 ½ ounces cacao beans
2/3 cup rice
1 cinnamon stick
1 tablespoon water
6 cups of milk
½ cup sugar
1 teaspoon vanilla
Ground cinnamon for garnish

Wash the rice and let it soak for 3-4 hours. Drain the rice. Wash and dry the cacao beans and toast them in a skillet for about 15-20 minutes until the shells are golden brown. In a food processor, blend the toasted cacao beans, soaked rice, cinnamon sticks and 1 tablespoon water until the texture is smooth. Then, add the milk, sugar and vanilla and blend once more. Serve over ice and garnish with ground cinnamon.

Cacao is a traditional Nicaraguan drink, akin to a chocolate variety of the Mexican horchata.

Serves 4.

Thanks to Chef Doña Pinita for contributing her recipe and supporting women leaders in Belize and Nicaragua.

Doña Pinita is the envy of many a chef in Nicaragua. She runs her own restaurant and bakery, La Terraza Margarita. She became Managua's first female TV chef when she started hosting her cooking show six years ago. She's published 10 cookbooks with over 700 recipes. Her full name is María Josefina Gurdián Mántica, but everyone knows her simply as "Doña Pinita."

She started out small. In the 1980s, when wartime embargoes and blockades left Nicaragua's supermarket shelves empty, she started baking and selling cookies out of her kitchen. She joined a bakery cooperative, banding together with other women in order to buy ingredients. The business grew, and eventually her home bakery turned into a full-service restaurant.

Even though La Terraza Margarita is one of Managua's best-known restaurants, Doña Pinita didn't forget where she started. She made a point to hire employees who were mostly housewives with scarce resources and no training. She trained each one herself in cooking, baking and food service, and now has 50 employees, some of whom have worked at La Terraza for more than 25 years.

Coffee Flan

Norma Gadea Paiva, Jinotega, Nicaragua

FOR THE CARAMELIZED TOPPING:
¾ cup sugar

FOR THE FLAN:
½ cup freshly brewed coffee
½ teaspoon vanilla extract
¼ teaspoon ground cinnamon
1 14-ounce can sweetened condensed milk
1 12-ounce can evaporated milk
6 eggs, beaten

Preheat the oven to 350 degrees.

Heat the sugar in a small saucepan over medium heat until it has melted and turned a deep golden brown, stirring it with a wooden spoon. Immediately pour it into a flan mold, tipping it quickly so that the caramel covers the bottom and halfway up the sides, coating evenly. Set aside.

Make the coffee and allow to cool to room temperature. Pour the coffee into a mixing bowl, and add the vanilla extract, cinnamon, condensed milk, evaporated milk and beaten eggs. Pour mixture into the flan mold. Lightly grease the inside of the flan mold lid and cover the flan. If you do not have a flan mold, use a round metal pan and cover the flan with aluminum foil.

Place the pan or flan mold in a roasting pan and pour hot water into the roasting pan, about halfway up the side of the mold.

Bake at 350 degrees for about 1 hour, or until the sides of the flan are set (the center will still move slightly when shaken gently).

Remove the pan from the water bath, remove the lid or foil and run a knife around the edges. Allow the flan to cool on a wire rack for 40 minutes. Refrigerate the flan for at least 4 hours and up to a day ahead.

Set the flan pan into hot water to loosen for 30 seconds, then invert onto a serving plate. Garnish with whipped cream if desired. Serves 6-8.

Thanks to Norma Gadea Paiva for contributing her recipe, and Equal Exchange UK, a fair trade organization which promotes all-female farming cooperatives in Latin America, for supporting women leaders in Belize and Nicaragua.

Ginger Hibiscus Punch

Sandra Felix, Belize City, Belize

4 cups dried hibiscus leaves (also called Flor de Jamaica or Sorrel)
1 cup fresh ginger root, peeled and sliced
4 quarts water, divided
Sugar or other sweetener

Add hibiscus leaves to 3 quarts boiling water and let sit for 10 minutes. Strain to remove leaves. Place the peeled and sliced ginger in a blender with the other quart of water to puree. Strain ginger and collect the water in large pitcher. Combine hibiscus and ginger liquids and add sugar or sweetener to taste. Chill in refrigerator or add ice and serve. Depending on how strong you like the flavors, you can add more or less water to taste.

Serves 8-10.

Thanks to Sandra Felix for contributing her recipe and supporting women leaders in Belize and Nicaragua.

Norma Elena is an organic coffee farmer and member of the all-women Soppexcca Coffee Co-operative in Jinotega, Nicaragua. Each member of Soppexcca is required to own her own plot of land, so she can make decisions independently and without anyone else's approval. When Norma joined the co-op eight years ago, there were five women members. Today 283 female farmers grow coffee and earn a living wage for themselves and their families. Norma and her colleagues started a national women's network of coffee farmers called "Flores de Café: Mujeres Unidas por Un Futuro Mejor," (The Coffee Flowers: Women United for A Better Future). Together they organize workshops and trainings to develop women leaders within cooperatives across Nicaragua. "It's important to make women's work visible," Norma said. "We want to give value to the important work that women do and which has traditionally been ignored. We no longer want to be forgotten."

More than 30,000 Nicaraguans earn their livelihoods from coffee production, the country's biggest export.

Blonde Fudge

Marla Magaña, Progresso, Belize

2 cans sweetened condensed milk
3 ½ cups sugar
2 tablespoons vanilla
½ cup peanuts, chopped
½ cup raisins (optional)

Grease a large flat pan with butter or vegetable oil. Heat the condensed milk in a saucepan on low heat. Add sugar and vanilla and stir constantly to prevent sticking and burning. Cook and stir until it barely boils and turns a medium brown color. Add peanuts and raisins.

To make sure the mixture is ready, check the sides of the pan to see if the mixture sticks and gets dry. Alternatively, you can add a drop of the mixture into a glass of water, and if it doesn't mix in and the water remains clear, then it is ready. Pour the mixture into the greased pan and spread evenly to approximately a ½-inch thickness. Let it cool and cut into squares while it is still warm (if it hardens, cutting it will be difficult).

Serves 8.

Thanks to Marla Magaña of Progresso, Belize, for contributing her recipe and supporting women leaders in Belize and Nicaragua.

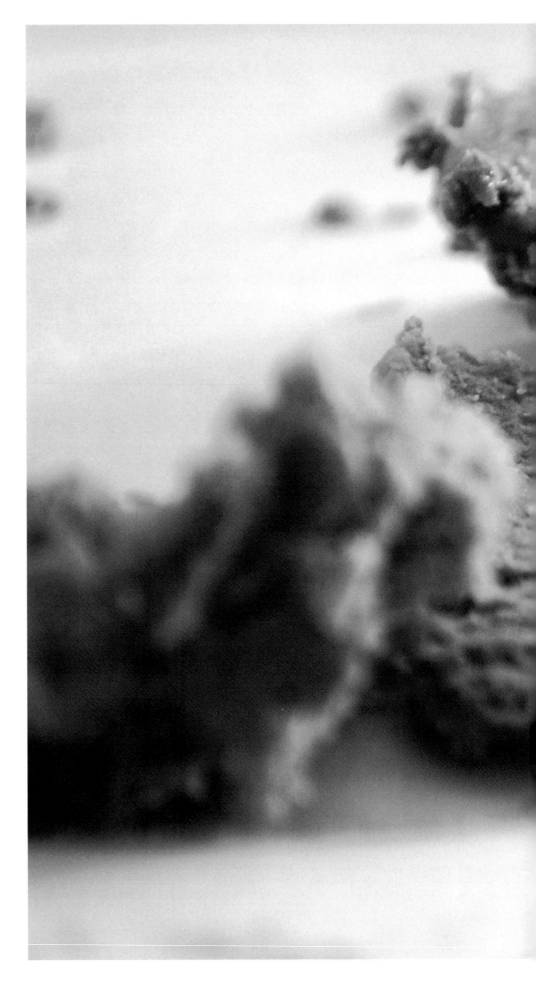

Nancy sits on her front porch, overlooking her son at play with a friend.

Nancy is a budding entrepreneur. Unable to afford childcare for her two children, she decided to build a business from home to better support her family. She started baking cakes and making party decorations for all the birthdays, anniversaries, weddings and quinceañeras in her community.

As her business grows, she plans to buy a bigger mixer and a larger oven to maximize production and cater larger events. "My work is an inheritance for my children," she says. She also wants to expand her business so that she can generate employment for other women in her community.

This is one of Nancy's most popular recipes.

Tres Leches Cake

Nancy Bermudez Notis, Bluefields, Nicaragua

1 ½ cups cake flour
3/4 cup sugar
1 teaspoon baking powder
1 stick butter, softened
6 eggs
1 cup whole milk
1 cup sweetened condensed milk
1 cup evaporated milk
1 teaspoon nutmeg
1 teaspoon vanilla

FROSTING
2 cups heavy whipping cream
2/3 cup sugar
1 teaspoon vanilla
1 teaspoon grated lime zest
  (optional)
Cherries or raisins (for garnish)

Preheat the oven to 350 degrees. In an electric mixer on low speed, beat the butter and sugar until well blended. Add the eggs one at a time while mixing, and add the vanilla. Add the dry ingredients – cake flour, nutmeg, and baking powder. Pour the batter into a greased baking pan and bake 30 minutes, or until the top is golden brown.

Remove from oven and set aside to cool. Pierce cake multiple times with a fork. In a separate bowl, mix the whole, condensed, and evaporated milks together. Pour the mixture over the whole cake.

Refrigerate cake from 2 to 8 hours, or until liquid is completely absorbed.

To make the frosting, beat the cream, sugar and vanilla together in an electric mixer until the mixture forms stiff peaks. Add the lime zest. Frost the cake and garnish with a few cherries or raisins.

Serves 10-12.

Progresso Bread Pudding

Chef Dulce María Durán, Laguna Grill, Progresso, Belize

2 loaves sliced bread (dipped in water, then squeezed to remove excess water)
1 can condensed milk
1 can evaporated milk
1/2 cup butter (melted)
2 teaspoons vanilla
2 teaspoons cinnamon powder
1 cup sugar
1 cup raisins
2 ounces rum (optional)

Mix all ingredients in a large bowl until well blended. Pour into greased baking pan or Pyrex baking dish. Bake on 350° for 45 minutes to an hour. Remove when top is golden brown.

Serves 10-12.

Thanks to Chef Dulce María Durán for contributing her recipe and supporting women leaders in Belize and Nicaragua.

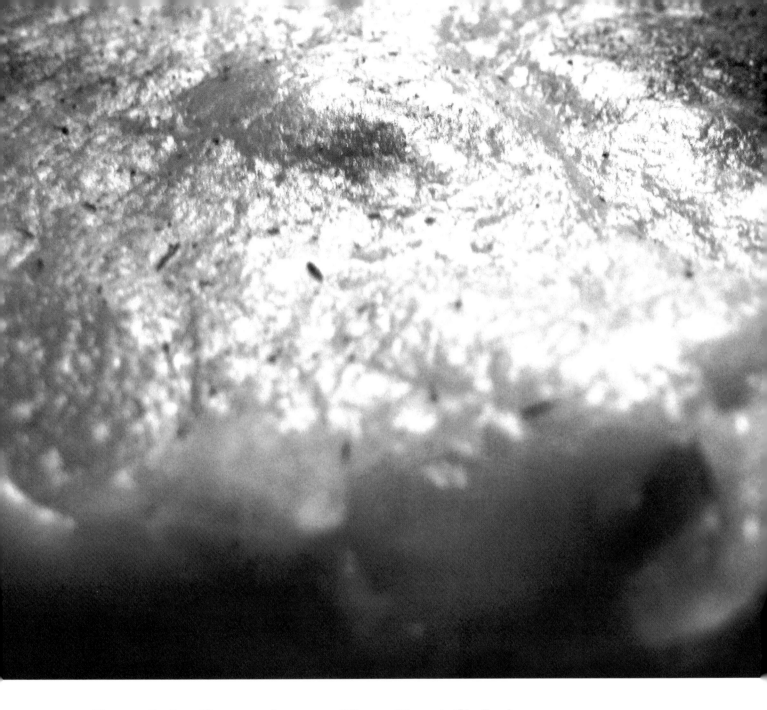

Pastel de Quequisque (Taro Root Cake)

Nancy Bermudez Notis, Bluefields, Nicaragua

Pastel de quequisque is a delicious Caribbean flourless and gluten-free delicacy. Accordingly, even though it is called "cake", its consistency is really more pudding-like. Keep baking it until the entire "cake" is set—this can take a long time but is worth the wait!

12 small quequisques (or taro roots), approximately 2 pounds
1/2 teaspoon salt
3 cups coconut milk
1 tablespoon ground ginger (optional)

3 cups sugar
3/4 stick of butter
2 teaspoons of ground cinnamon (divided)
2 teaspoons vanilla extract

Preheat the oven to 350 degrees. Wash and peel the quequisques. Cut them into cubes and boil them for 8 minutes until soft.

Next, blend the cubed quequisques in a food processor with the coconut milk, sugar, salt, melted butter, vanilla, ginger, and 1 teaspoon of the cinnamon. Process until mixed well.

Pour mixture into a 9" x 13" glass baking dish and bake for about 80-100 minutes. The cake is finished when the top is golden brown and a toothpick inserted into various parts of the cake comes out cleanly. Remove from oven, dust cake with the remaining teaspoon of cinnamon, let cool and serve. The cake will also firm up more after refrigeration.

Serves 10-12.

Papaya Punch

Daisy Magaña, Progresso, Belize

Choosing a papaya can be tricky. Ripe papayas have yellow skin and are slightly soft (but not squishy) to the touch. If ripe papayas aren't available, simply put a green papaya in a paper bag on the counter for a few days until the skin turns yellow.

1 ripe papaya
1 can evaporated milk
4 cups of water
½ cup sugar (optional)

Cut the papaya in half and remove all the seeds. Remove the skin from the papaya and cut the fruit into small pieces. Blend the papaya with the water and evaporated milk. Add sugar a little at a time, to taste. Depending on how ripe the papaya is, you may not need any sugar at all.

Serves 4.

Thanks to Daisy Magaña for contributing her recipe and supporting women leaders in Belize and Nicaragua.

Macúa de Nicaragua (Nicaraguan Rum Cocktail)

2 ounces White Rum (Flor de Caña* is the leading Nicaraguan brand)
2 ounces guava juice
1 ounce orange juice
1 ounce lemon juice
Slice of orange for garnish

Shake all ingredients together and serve over ice. Garnish with a slice of orange.

Yields one serving.

* Flor de Caña is the leading Nicaraguan brand of rum. It's known as one of the best rums produced in Latin America, and it has won more than 100 international awards since 2000, more than any other brand of rum.

The macúa, named after a tropical bird of Nicaragua, is the country's national drink.

Quequisques are starchy root vegetables, close cousins of the vegetables called cocoyams (or taro roots in the United States). Cassava and yucca can be substituted if quequisques or taro roots can't be found.

Pío Quinto (Rum and Custard Cake)

Doña Pinita, Owner and Chef, La Terraza Margarita Restaurant, Managua, Nicaragua

CAKE*

4 eggs
1 cup sugar
2 cups flour
1 ½ teaspoon baking powder
¼ cup milk
½ teaspoon of vanilla
1 pinch of salt

*you can also substitute 1 package of white or yellow plain cake mix and follow preparation directions

SYRUP

1 cup sugar
¾ cup water
1 cinnamon stick
½ teaspoon of lime juice
¼ cup rum
1 teaspoon whole cloves
½ cup raisins
8 prunes

ATOLILLO (SIMPLE CUSTARD)

2 cups milk
½ cup sugar
1 egg yolk
2 ½ tablespoons cornstarch

1 cinnamon stick
Ground cinnamon

PREPARING THE CAKE:

Preheat the oven to 350 degrees. Grease a square 8"x8" baking pan and dust with flour. Sift together the dry ingredients (flour, baking soda and salt). Beat the eggs with the sugar and vanilla for 10 minutes on high speed. Gently fold the dry ingredients into the wet ingredients (eggs, sugar, and vanilla). Pour the batter into the baking dish. Bake at 350 degrees for approximately 30 minutes.

PREPARING THE SYRUP:

Put the sugar, water, rum, cinnamon stick, cloves and lime juice in a heavy-bottomed saucepan over medium-high heat. Stir mixture slowly until it reaches a boil and then remove the cloves and cinnamon stick. Add the raisins and prunes and let simmer for a few minutes until the liquid reduces and forms a syrup. Remove the syrup from the heat and let cool.

PREPARING THE ATOLILLO:

Add one cup of milk, the sugar and cinnamon stick in a heavy-bottomed saucepan over low heat. Before the mixture boils, dissolve the cornstarch in half a cup of milk and add to the saucepan. Then, add the egg yolk to the final half-cup of milk and add to the saucepan as well. Stir consistently and slowly until the mixture has thickened. When the mixture has thickened, remove from heat and take out the cinnamon stick.

Once the cake has cooled, pour the cooled syrup over the cake, reserving some of the raisins and all of the prunes. Let cake absorb the syrup for a few minutes and then pour the atolillo over the moistened cake. Decorate with ground cinnamon and reserved raisins and prunes. Cool before serving.

Thanks to Chef Doña Pinita for contributing her recipe and supporting women leaders in Belize and Nicaragua. See Doña Pinita's story, p. 81.

Gifiti, a bitter Garifuna tradition

Gifiti is a medicinal drink believed to have potent healing powers. Made by steeping a variety of herbs in alcohol, this bitter drink is said to cure ailments like fevers and upset stomachs, and even enhance sexual performance.

Created by the Garifuna people, an ethnic minority in Belize, this elixir's recipe varies from place to place, and is usually passed down within families. Typically made from rum and a variety of herbs and roots, some recipes can include dozens of other ingredients including flowers, seeds, leaves, branches and bark. Most Gifiti includes garlic (a natural immune system booster), allspice (a blood tonic), jícaro negro (roots of a black nut-bearing tree used for calming the nervous system) and cinnamon and cloves for flavoring.

All the ingredients are packed tightly into a large bottle and covered in rum. The bottle can be refilled multiple times, depending on the ingredients, and can last up to a year.

Learn more about our partner organizations.

Bringing Nutrition to Every Family: Addressing Food Security in Nicaragua and Belize, p. 95

4-H at work in Progresso, Belize, p. 96

WIN Belize at work in Belize City, Belize, p. 97

Other organizations advancing women's rights in Belize, p. 97

Fabretto Children's Foundation at work across Nicaragua, p. 98

OMAN at work in Bluefields, Nicaragua, p. 99

Other organizations advancing women's rights in Nicaragua, p. 99

Kitchen Leader Lilia Ack's family, L-R: her daughter Yanira and grandson Sergio; son Carmelito and daughter Fabiola. Right: Cows on a Mennonite farm outside Progresso, Belize.

Bringing Nutrition to Every Family:
Addressing Food Security in Nicaragua and Belize

Food security exists when all people within a community have consistent access to nutritional foods that allow them to live healthy lives. Three elements are key to food security. Sufficient quantities of food must be available, food must be economically and physically accessible, and residents must be able to use food properly, practicing adequate sanitation and nutritional care. Many parts of Nicaragua and Belize are "food-insecure," however, and it's still a challenge for households to obtain enough healthy food to sustain themselves.

Approximately 45% of Nicaragua's 5.7 million people live in extreme poverty on less than $1 a day, according to USAID. Malnutrition is high, especially in the region of Madriz, the northwestern corridor of Nicaragua. The harsh dry climate, low-tech food production and extreme poverty all serve as roadblocks for families trying to access enough healthy food. Even when nutritional foods are available in these communities, sometimes families simply don't know which foods are healthier than others.

The Fabretto Children's Foundation is working to address food insecurity in Nicaragua. Fabretto provides school lunches with all the vital proteins, vitamins, and minerals students' diets lack. Mothers of the students volunteer to prepare the lunches, earning valuable skills while more fully engaging in their children's education. Fabretto also promotes school and family gardens for students, teachers, and families to learn small-scale production of nutritious foods. To optimize local resources, sustainable and organic techniques are used. Parents volunteer in the gardens, learning how to grow fruits and vegetables for their own families.

Belize's biggest industry is tourism, and so despite arable land and favorable climate conditions, there hasn't been much investment in infrastructure for local food production. Belize relies heavily on imported food, and it's often prohibitively expensive for local families.

More than 20% of Belizean youth ages 15-24 are unemployed. 4-H sees an opportunity for young people to help Belize adopt better farming technologies in the future. For 50 years, 4-H clubs throughout Belize have equipped at-risk youth with skills to work in agriculture and food preparation. Not only do youth learn marketable skills to feed their families, they're part of the solution to achieve food security in Belize.

Special thanks to Peter Schaller, Director of Communications and Strategy at the Fabretto Children's Foundation, for contributing to this piece.

4-H at work in Progresso, Belize

Progresso 4-H volunteers gather at the Laguna Grill for a celebration.

Because public school in Belize is not free and can be too costly for many families, many Belizeans cannot afford to finish high school. That's where 4-H steps in. 4-H equips at-risk Belizean youth with skills to work in agriculture, food preparation, building technology, and tourism.

Each year, Belizean youth 14-19 who are not enrolled in school can participate in a 10-month 4-H program. They learn small-scale livestock production (pigs, goats and chickens), vegetable production and sanitary food preparation. 4-H tackles two problems at once – youth unemployment and community access to nutrition. When young people learn how to cultivate their own food, the whole community benefits. Children teach their parents the skills they learn, and small gardens turn into backyard family farms, providing enough food to feed the family as well as generating extra income.

Youth looking to start their own business get entrepreneurial training, and 4-H graduates get job placement assistance. 4-H also helps students who wish to return to school high school after leaving. They fundraise throughout the year to offer scholarships to participants, and provide application assistance and tutoring. In addition to equipping youth with marketable skills, 4-H also runs a number of recreational and cultural activities, including sports, arts and crafts, community service, music, dance, and gardening.

The Progresso 4-H club is especially active and emphasizes community service. Youth and their families work together to clear trash and brush from the town's lagoon, and hold regular fundraisers to help pay 4-H club members' high school fees.

WIN Belize at work in Belize City, Belize

WIN Belize is a network of 18 organizations working together to improve the lives of women in Belize. Individually, WIN Belize's member organizations focus on issues including teenage pregnancy, HIV/AIDS, sexual and reproductive health, commercial sexual exploitation, gender-based violence, and women's economic empowerment and leadership. As a coalition, WIN Belize advocates for policies that advance the rights of women and children.

Over the years, WIN Belize has strengthened local organizations through fundraising, training and staff development. It partners with smaller NGOs in Belize to provide logistical help in implementing women's empowerment projects. In 2005, WIN Belize led a successful campaign to both raise the minimum wage and eliminate wage disparities between men and women.

WIN Belize recently launched a two-year initiative to encourage women to participate in electoral politics. Very few women hold decision-making roles in the government, and cultural and social barriers have long deterred many women from seeking leadership positions. Only 6 out of the 43 members of Belize's National Assembly are women. But with funding from the United Nations Development Programme, WIN Belize aims to strengthen women's representation in national leadership roles. WIN Belize trains women in public speaking, reviewing and revising legislation, and running a successful campaign.

Other organizations advancing women's rights in Belize

Belize Family Life Association (BFLA): BFLA provides sexual and reproductive health services and education to Belizeans of all ages.

Belize Rural Women's Association (BRWA): The BRWA provides cooperatives of rural women with the financial resources needed to access means of production, materials and related business-development services.

CARE-Belize: CARE-Belize assists families with children who have disabilities, providing training and rehabilitation support.

Chairladies Fajina Association: CFA is a cooperative of Mayan craftswomen from 20 villages who have been working together to market their unique basketry, embroidery, and other handiwork at a small storefront in Punta Gorda.

Haven House: Haven House provides shelter and support services for women and their children who are survivors of domestic violence.

LEAP Belize (Leading and Empowering Others in Action and Principles): LEAP helps single mothers improve their parenting skills, continue their education and learn marketable skills to generate income.

Plenty Belize: Plenty Belize, located in Punta Gorda in the south of Belize, assists primary schools in developing organic gardens and volunteer-run lunch programs to combat the area's persistent problem of malnutrition. They also issue micro-loans for small-scale economic development projects for single mothers and families.

Productive Organisation for Women in Action (POWA): In 2003, a group of Belizean women came together in response to the rapid spread of HIV in their communities. They formed POWA, the Productive Organisation for Women in Action. Members educate their communities about sexual and reproductive health and advocate to end gender-based violence and inequality. POWA

also empowers Belizean women with marketable skills, like artisanal craft-making.

PSI/PASMO Belize: PSI/PASMO Belize uses targeted research and innovative social marketing strategies to prevent the spread of HIV/AIDS and foster sexual and reproductive health in communities throughout Belize. In order to direct resources where they are most needed, PSI/PASMO targets the most at-risk and vulnerable populations and tailors strategies to reach each respective group. PSI is a multi-partner initiative supported by the Global Fund to Fight AIDS, the United Nations, USAID and many other Belizean and international NGOs.

Regina Martinez Foundation: Women of the Jane Usher Boulevard neighborhood in Belize City came together to form the Regina Martinez Foundation. The members have organized to lobby for additional park space for neighborhood children and street lights for the neighborhood, which currently suffers from some of the highest crime in Belize City. The Foundation has also organized a small sewing cooperative to enable their members to earn income.

Youth Enhancement Services (YES): YES advocates for young women and girls in Belize through a variety of programs. In addition to providing education and vocational training to young women, YES offers support services for teenage mothers and works to prevent the spread of HIV/AIDS. YES has also led several public awareness campaigns to end sexual abuse and commercial sexual exploitation.

YWCA-Belize: The YWCA offers a number of programs for women in Belize, including free and low-cost daycare, literacy education and vocational training. The H.E.L.P. program, or the Helping Early Leavers Program, provides supplemental education and career skills training to girls ages 13-18 who cannot afford to attend high school.

Fabretto Children's Foundation at work across Nicaragua

The Fabretto Children's Foundation helps underprivileged Nicaraguan children and their families escape poverty and reach their full potential. Fabretto serves approximately 10,500 children and their families from six Fabretto centers and more than 50 public elementary schools. Students enrolled in Fabretto programs receive nutritious lunches, educational reinforcement, and basic health and hygiene education. Without Fabretto, many of these children would otherwise have to drop out of school to take care of younger siblings or work to help support their families.

The NicaHOPE jewelry project, founded in 2008 as an entrepreneurial initiative of Fabretto, provides vocational training and alternative income-generation to youth from the community in and around La Chureca, the Managua city trash dump. Children in the community often live in unsafe conditions, working in the dump and earning less than $3 a day. The jewelry project aims to provide these youth with alternative opportunities for sustainable, healthy, and dignified work. Fabretto offers a variety of other critical programs to La Chureca's residents, including computer classes, tutoring and support services for at-risk youth, and school lunch programs that serve about 2,000 students a day.

To learn more, visit www.fabretto.org.

NicaHOPE artisans use beads, wood, stone, wire, glass and recycled materials to make beautiful and complex pieces. Check out NicaHOPE handcrafted jewelry in the Fabretto online store: http://fabretto. donorshops. com/products/ jewelry.php.

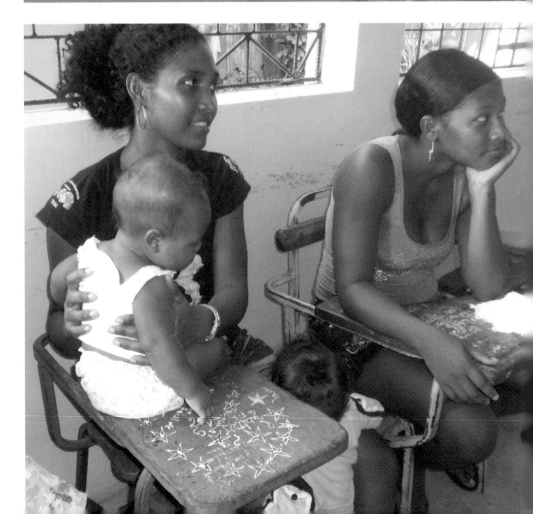

OMAN at work in Bluefields, Nicaragua

OMAN, the Organization of Nicaraguan Women of African Descent, works to promote the identity, culture and traditions of the Afro-descendant population living along Nicaragua's Caribbean coast. OMAN empowers young women to advocate for a variety of social justice issues including promoting economic development, women's entrepreneurship and ending violence against women.

The Afro-Nicaraguan population has traditionally been marginalized compared to the majority Nicaraguan Mestizo population. Afro-Nicaraguans experience higher rates of unemployment, illiteracy and poverty. Teen pregnancy and drug abuse is a growing problem among Afro-descendant youth. Frustrated by the situation in their community, Zada Saphri and Gay Sturling started OMAN in 2000, and began to convene weekly meetings with other young women. They discussed themes like increased access to education, employment, and civic engagement.

OMAN recently received its official national designation as a registered nonprofit, and members have begun to attend training conferences to develop leadership and management skills.

Left: Members of OMAN meet for a discussion group.

Other organizations advancing women's rights in Nicaragua

Casa Alianza: Casa Alianza is an international non-governmental organization dedicated to the rehabilitation and defense of street children in Honduras, Nicaragua, Mexico and Guatemala. Each year, their crisis center in Nicaragua provides 5,000 children shelter, food, medical care, protection and mental health services. Casa Alianza also provides extensive family therapy and support services to single mothers. In 2000, Casa Alianza was the first Latin American organization to be awarded the Conrad N. Hilton Humanitarian Award.

Centro de Mujeres Xochilt-Acalt: The Xochilt-Acalt Ccenter began as a sexual and reproductive health clinic for women in Malpaisillo in 1990. The center has since grown and promotes other women's empowerment initiatives in addition to clinical services. Xochilt-Acalt teaches adult education and literacy classes, provides vocational training in agriculture, and runs a small business program.

Centro Para la Participacion Democratica y el Desarrollo (CENZONTLE): The Center for Democratic Participation and Development aims to improve socioeconomic conditions among poor Nicaraguan women by pro-viding skills training and developing sustainable microenterprise proj-ects in their communities.

Comité de Mujeres Rurales: The Committee of Rural Women empowers women economically by training them to run their own agricultural enterprises. Women learn to raise sheep and goats and receive training on efficient irrigation methods and farming practices to grow crops in their own yards.

Cooperativa de Mujeres Nueva Vida: After Hurricane Mitch hit Nicaragua in 1998, many people who had lost their homes found their way to the Nueva Vida refugee camp. To begin rebuilding their livelihoods, women from the Nueva Vida refugee community formed a sewing cooperative. After they received a few donated sewing machines and six months of sewing classes, the women got to work. The cooperative grew and began taking orders. Now, the cooperative is able to give work to 140 women.

FADCANIC: FADCANIC (Foundation for the Autonomy and Development of the Atlantic Coast of Nicaragua) works on several community development projects, including the promotion of sustainable agroforestry and increasing primary school bilingual education for indigenous and ethnic peoples on the Caribbean coast. The organization often works in conjunction with USAID and other international NGOs.

Fondo Para el Desarrollo de la Mujer (FODEM): The Fund for the Development of Women supports women entrepreneurs by giving small business training and microloans. With FODEM's support, women have opened small stores and restaurants and started small enterprises selling clothing or crafts.

INPHRU Casa de Las Niñas: INPHRU works with vulnerable children and young people to help them determine their own future. The Casa de Las Niñas Project provides safe shelter, counseling, training, and legal advocacy for girls who have been sexually and/or physically abused.

National Coalition Against Human Trafficking: In 2004, 35 different organizations came together to fight human trafficking more effectively in Nicaragua. The coalition consists of multilateral organizations like the United Nations Children's Fund (UNICEF) and the International Organization for Migration (IOM); government entities including the Nicaraguan Attorney General's office, Customs and Immigration, and the Ministry for the Family; and local NGO's including the Children's Coalition and the Women's Association. The coalition has compiled cases that have led to more successful prosecutions of traffickers and increased support for trafficked victims.

Recipe Index

BREADS & BISCUITS
Corn Tortillas, p. 58
Flour Tortillas, p. 58
Johnny Cakes (Breakfast Biscuits), p. 22
Powder Buns, p. 20

BREAKFASTS
Coconut Milk Pancakes with Bananas and
    Walnuts, p. 23
Garden Tofu Quiche with Vegetables, p. 21
Huevos Revueltos (Scrambled Eggs) with
    Chorizo and Avocado, p. 18
Johnny Cakes (Breakfast Biscuits), p. 22
Powder Buns, p. 20

BEANS AND LEGUMES
Coconut Rice and Beans, p. 60
Gallo Pinto, p. 16
Garnachas (Tostadas with Beans), p. 29
Split Peas and Pig Tails, p. 44

BEEF
Carne Asada, p. 69
Enchiladas (Fried Empanadas Filled with
    Meat and Rice), p. 30
Escabeche (Spicy Stew with Chicken
    and Onions), p. 46
Indio Viejo (Beef and Vegetable Stew),
    p. 41
Mini Pizzas, p. 27
Run Down (Caribbean Soup of Meat,
    Coconut Milk and Vegetables), p. 45
Sopa de Albóndigas (Chicken and Squash
    Meatball Stew), p. 40

CHICKEN
Arroz de la Valenciana (Rice with Chicken
    and Vegetables), p. 71
Chicken Tamales Wrapped in Banana
    Leaves, p. 67
Chimole (Black Stew), p. 42
Curry Chicken, p. 73
Escabeche (Spicy Stew with Chicken and
    Onions), p. 46
Frito (Fried Chicken atop Tangy Cabbage
    Slaw and Plantain Chips), p. 74
Pilau Rice, p. 50
Run Down (Caribbean Soup of Meat,
    Coconut Milk and Vegetables), p. 45
Salbutes (Fried Tortillas with Chicken,
    Tomatoes and Cabbage), p. 28
Stew Chicken, p. 70
Sopa de Albóndigas (Chicken and Squash
    Meatball Stew), p. 40

DESSERTS
Blonde Fudge, p. 84
Bread Pudding, p. 87
Coffee Flan, p. 82
Tres Leches Cake, p. 86

Pastel de Quequisque (Taro Root Cake),
    p. 88
Pio Quinto (Rum and Custard Cake), p. 90
Pudín de Camote (Sweet Potato Pudding),
    p. 78

DRINKS
Fresco de Cacao (Chocolate Rice Milk
    Drink), p. 81
Ginger Hibiscus Punch, p. 83
Horchata (Sweet Rice Milk Drink), p. 80
Macúa de Nicaragua (Rum Cocktail), p. 89
Papaya Punch, p. 89

EGGS
Huevos Revueltos (Scrambled Eggs) with
    Chorizo and Avocado, p. 18
Garden Tofu Quiche with Vegetables, p. 21
Guacamole with Hard-boiled Eggs, p. 33
Potato and Egg Salad, p. 52

PORK
Mini Pizzas, p. 27
Split Peas and Pig Tails, p. 44
Vigorón (Fried Yucca Topped with Fried
    Pork Rind and Cabbage Slaw), p. 72

RICE
Arroz de la Valenciana (Rice with Chicken
    and Vegetables), p. 71
Coconut Rice and Beans, p. 60
Gallo Pinto, p. 16
Pilau Rice, p. 50

SALADS & SIDES
Cabbage Slaw, p. 74
Coconut Rice and Beans, p. 60
Darasa (Garifuna Banana and Coconut
    Dumplings), p. 53
Gallo Pinto, p. 16
Guacamole with Hard-boiled Eggs, p. 33
Enchiladas (Fried Empanadas Filled with
    Meat and Rice), p. 30
Hudut (Mashed Plantains), p. 39
Maduros en Gloria (Sweet Baked
    Plantains), p. 54
Pilau Rice, p. 50
Plantain Chips, p. 57
Potato and Egg Salad, p. 52
Salbutes (Fried Tortillas with Chicken,
    Tomatoes and Cabbage), p. 28
Shrimp Ceviche, p. 33
Spicy Habanero and Cabbage Relish, p. 68

SEAFOOD
Garlic-Lime Snapper, p. 73
Hudut with Falumou (Garifuna Fish and
    Coconut Stew with Mashed Plantains),
    p. 38
Pilau Rice, p. 50
Shrimp Ceviche, p. 33

SOUPS
Chimole (Black Stew), p. 42
Escabeche (Spicy Stew with Chicken and
    Onions), p. 46
Hudut with Falumou (Garifuna Fish and
    Coconut Stew with Mashed Plantains),
    p. 38
Indio Viejo (Beef and Vegetable Stew),
    °p. 41
Run Down (Caribbean Soup of Meat,
    Coconut Milk and Vegetables), p. 45
Sopa de Albóndigas (Chicken and Squash
    Meatball Stew), p. 40
Split Peas and Pig Tails, p. 44

SPICES AND SAUCES
Marie Sharp's Hot Sauce, p. 68
Red Recado Spice Blend, p. 68
Spicy Habanero and Cabbage Relish, p. 68

VEGETARIAN
Blonde Fudge, p. 84
Bread Pudding, p. 87
Cabbage Slaw, p. 74
Coconut Milk Pancakes with Bananas and
    Walnuts, p. 23
Coconut Rice and Beans, p. 60
Coffee Flan, p. 82
Corn Tortillas, p. 58
Darasa (Garifuna Banana and Coconut
    Dumplings), p. 53
Enchiladas (Fried Empanadas Filled with
    Meat and Rice), p. 30
Flour Tortillas, p. 58
Fresco de Cacao (Chocolate Rice Milk
    Drink), p. 81
Gallo Pinto, p. 16
Garden Tofu Quiche with Vegetables, p. 21
Garnachas (Tostadas with Beans), p. 29
Ginger Hibiscus Punch, p. 83
Guacamole with Hard-boiled Eggs, p. 33
Horchata (Sweet Rice Milk Drink), p. 80
Hudut (Mashed Plantains), p. 39
Johnny Cakes (Breakfast Biscuits), p. 22
Macúa de Nicaragua (Rum Cocktail), p. 89
Maduros en Gloria (Sweet Baked
    Plantains), p. 54
Papaya Punch, p. 89
Pastel de Quequisque (Taro Root Cake),
    p. 88
Pilau Rice, p. 50
Pio Quinto (Rum and Custard Cake), p. 90
Plantain Chips, p. 57
Potato and Egg Salad, p. 52
Powder Buns, p. 20
Pudín de Camote (Sweet Potato Pudding),
    p. 78
Red Recado Spice Blend, p. 68
Spicy Habanero and Cabbage Relish, p. 68
Tres Leches Cake, p. 86

The Leaders from the Kitchen production team would like to thank all the women who contributed their recipes and stories to this book. We would also like to thank the following people and organizations for their generous support.

IN BELIZE
4-H Club of Progresso, Belize
Chef Esther from Changes in
  Latitude, San Pedro Belize
Chef Walt, Dulce and Mr. Harold
  at the Laguna Grill
Ernie at Captain Morgan's Resort
GoJoven
Jeff Spiegel at Azul Resort/Rojo
  Lounge
The Magaña Family
Mary and Erica Dahlquist at
  Belizean Shores
Regina Martinez Foundation
Sandra Felix
WIN Belize

IN CHICAGO
Belizean Cultural Heritage
  Association
Citizen Bridges International
Erica Marten Photography
Garifuna Flava
Jason Kaumeyer
Jessica Huang
John King
Melissa Guzicki
Sol Ennis, Blackfreighter
  Productions
Tiffanie Beatty
The U.S. State Department

IN NICARAGUA
Casa Alianza
Carlos Olivas
Doña Pinita at La Terraza Margarita
Esperanza Pereira
Fabretto Childern's Foundation
Jelissa Pineda
Mallory Erickson, NicaHOPE
Maryeling Murillo, NicaHOPE
OMAN, the Organization of
  Nicaraguan Women of African
  Descent
Peter Schaller at Fabretto
Xiomara Ibarra Zelaya

Meet the project team

Citizen Bridges' Emerging Belizean, Nicaraguan, & U.S. Leaders & Leaders from the Kitchen Project Team Members, from left to right, top to bottom: **Sarah Sumadi** (U.S.) and **Jamie Hayes** (U.S.); **Jamie Peterson** (U.S.); **Daisy Magaña** (Belize); **Marcela Perez** (Nicaragua); **Megan Hryndza** (U.S.); **Indira Bartley** (Belize); **Lestell Kelly** (Nicaragua)

CPSIA information can be obtained
at www.ICGtesting.com
Printed in the USA
LVIC04n0215281114
415979LV00004B/5